SOLOMON'S
ANGELS

Also by Doreen Virtue, Ph.D.

Books/Kits/Oracle Board

ANGEL NUMBERS 101
MY GUARDIAN ANGEL (with Amy Oscar)
ANGEL BLESSINGS CANDLE KIT (with Grant Virtue)
(includes booklet, CD, journal, etc.)
HOW TO HEAR YOUR ANGELS
HEALING WORDS FROM THE ANGELS
FAIRIES 101
REALMS OF THE EARTH ANGELS
DIVINE MAGIC
HOW TO GIVE AN ANGEL CARD READING KIT
ANGELS 101
ANGEL GUIDANCE BOARD
GODDESSES & ANGELS
CRYSTAL THERAPY (with Judith Lukomski)
CONNECTING WITH YOUR ANGELS KIT
(includes booklet, CD, journal, etc.)
ANGEL MEDICINE
THE CRYSTAL CHILDREN
ARCHANGELS & ASCENDED MASTERS
EARTH ANGELS
MESSAGES FROM YOUR ANGELS
ANGEL VISIONS II
EATING IN THE LIGHT (with Becky Prelitz, M.F.T., R.D.)
THE CARE AND FEEDING OF INDIGO CHILDREN
HEALING WITH THE FAIRIES
ANGEL VISIONS
DIVINE PRESCRIPTIONS
HEALING WITH THE ANGELS
"I'D CHANGE MY LIFE IF I HAD MORE TIME"
DIVINE GUIDANCE
CHAKRA CLEARING
(available in tradepaper, and as a hardcover book-with-CD)
ANGEL THERAPY
THE LIGHTWORKER'S WAY
CONSTANT CRAVING A–Z
CONSTANT CRAVING
THE YO-YO DIET SYNDROME
LOSING YOUR POUNDS OF PAIN

SOLOMON'S
ANGELS

Doreen Virtue, Ph.D.

HAY HOUSE, INC.
Carlsbad, California • New York City
London • Sydney • Johannesburg
Vancouver • Hong Kong • New Delhi

Published and distributed in the United States by: Hay House, Inc.: www.hayhouse.com • *Published and distributed in Australia by:* Hay House Australia Pty. Ltd.: www.hayhouse.com.au • *Published and distributed in the United Kingdom by:* Hay House UK, Ltd.: www.hayhouse.co.uk • *Published and distributed in the Republic of South Africa by:* Hay House SA (Pty), Ltd.: www.hayhouse.co.za • *Distributed in Canada by:* Raincoast: www.raincoast.com • *Published in India by:* Hay House Publishers India: www.hayhouse.co.in

Editorial supervision: Jill Kramer • *Design:* Tricia Breidenthal • *Interior illustrations:* Marius Michael-George

Library of Congress Cataloging-in-Publication Data

Virtue, Doreen.
 Solomon's angels / Doreen Virtue. -- 1st ed.
    p. cm.
 ISBN 978-1-4019-1786-9
 1. Solomon, King of Israel--Fiction. 2. Angels--Fiction. 3. New Age fiction.
I. Title.
 PS3622.I785S67 2008
 813'.6--dc22

                           2007028533

ISBN: 978-1-4019-1786-9

11 10 09 08 5 4 3 2
1st edition, February 2008
2nd edition, February 2008

Printed in the United States of America

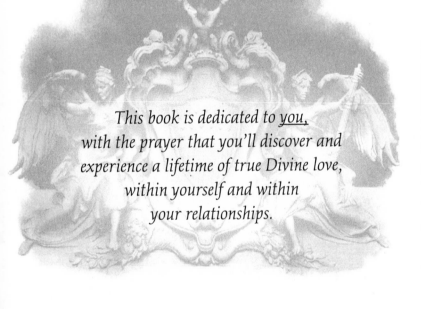

This book is dedicated to <u>you</u>,
with the prayer that you'll discover and
experience a lifetime of true Divine love,
within yourself and within
your relationships.

PREFACE

I've always been fascinated and inspired by powerful women who have changed the world, such as Joan of Arc, St. Bernadette of Lourdes, Mother Teresa, Amelia Earhart, and the American suffragettes Alice Paul and Lucy Burns.

The legends of the Queen of Sheba have long attracted me, with their tales of the young and beautiful woman who ruled over a vastly prosperous and peaceful nation and who traveled the long and arduous journey to visit the wise and magical King Solomon during the 10th century B.C.

My fascination with the history of spirituality and religion probably borders on an addictive obsession. Ninety percent of the books and videos in my personal library relate to that topic! I love reading the stories and learning about the archaeology of how various religions were birthed and nurtured.

Writing this book fed my passion for spending endless hours poring over ancient scriptures and texts—fact-checking and comparing Jewish, Yemeni, Ethiopian, Islamic, and other legends about King Solomon and the Queen of Sheba. Much of the information about these two celebrated figures is speculative, as there are only brief mentions of them in the Bible and in works by historians such as Josephus. Since actual biographical details about the Queen of Sheba and King Solomon are sparse, much of my research focused on legends from ancient Jewish texts; the Yemeni, Muslim, and Ethiopian cultures; and Freemasonry texts and lectures.

I felt like a detective as I pored over the controversies among experts on ancient Saba (the Queen of Sheba's commonwealth) and pieced together the names and identities of its pantheon of deities. The latest and most respected experts name Almaqah as the Sabaeans' sun god and chief deity, replacing previous theories that Almaqah was a minor deity or even a moon god or goddess.

During the writing of this book, I also received a great deal of information while sleeping. For example, I woke up from an afternoon nap to the sound of a male voice I recognized as Archangel Michael instructing me on the vibrational properties of the universe. I was pleased and amazed by how many times the information I received by osmosis later matched up with

the historical texts' accounts. So I synthesized all of that data into the background of this book's story.

The Queen of Sheba was a woman named Makeda (sometimes called Balquis or Balkis) who inherited the throne from her father when she was about sixteen years old. Her commonwealth, known as Saba' or Sheba, encompassed both the eastern and western regions of the landmass surrounding the southern tip of the Red Sea.

Saba's commonwealth was comprised of many tribes called *sha͏ᶜbs*, which were each led by *kabir qynm* or group leaders. These tribes were communal in nature, in that all property belonged to the entire tribe and not to individuals. The kabir qynm all answered to the king or queen of Saba, who was considered to be the supreme political leader of the commonwealth and who resided in the capital city of Ma'rib. The major cities of Aksum in Ethiopia and Ma'rib in Yemen still hold archaeological evidence of Saba's temples, palaces, and prosperity.

We know from biblical sources that the queen was a very beautiful black woman (although countless legends speak of the queen's misshapen feet and her connection to the Jinn elemental realm). The intelligence she possessed in ruling one of the most peaceful lands

of her time was also evident in her intention to test the wise King Solomon's knowledge by posing riddles to him.

The accounts of the mighty, charismatic, and powerful King Solomon usually focus on his wisdom and the famous story in which he boldly decided the fate of two women debating their rights to a baby. I avoided recounting the clichéd legends and concentrated on capturing the essence of a man who was born amid great turmoil within his household and kingdom. The ancient tales of his connection to the angels and birds were also essential to telling his story. In addition, King Solomon's profound Proverbs are sprinkled throughout.

The Freemasons also have their stories to tell about the powerful meeting of a king and queen, their love triangle with an architect, and the secrets of the Temple of Solomon's construction. All of these legends about King Solomon and the Queen of Sheba are woven together in these pages.

I want to thank Reid Tracy and Ileen Maisel for encouraging me to pen this book—it's a dream come true to write a historically based spiritual novel. I was surprised when I first sat down to draft the book and Queen Makeda's voice came through me, as I'd

planned on writing it from both royals' points of view. But as soon as she spoke, I knew that a first-person account was the right approach.

I'd heard from other authors that characters in a novel take on their own life and dictate the direction of the book. Well, that was certainly true in this one! The strong personalities of Queen Makeda, King Solomon, Tamrin, and the archangels took over any semblance of artistic control I had, beginning with page one. I just watched their actions, and described them as best I could.

I truly enjoyed writing this book, and my prayer is that you'll also enjoy it!

With love,
Doreen Virtue

CHAPTER 1

At first I fought for control of my emotions. <u>He doesn't matter,</u> I told myself, pretending to be aloof. I even willed my breathing and heartbeat to relax. But then I looked into his eyes, went limp, and surrendered.

His eyelashes danced with poetic intelligence and alert playfulness. My heart thumped against his chest as he pulled me into his sandalwood scent—I feared that its loudness betrayed the depth of my passion for him much too early in our relationship. My head filled with pleasure, then fear, then the sound of my own heartbeat. The loud sound continued. . . .

As I pulled back the gold silk comforter from over my head, dozens of brightly embroidered pillows spilled onto the floor. The noise continued as I groaned and opened my eyes reluctantly. I stared into the center of the round canopy hanging above me. Colored like a fiery sunset, its soft netting enveloped my bed like solar rays. On summer nights, that netting was the only thing that kept the biting insects away.

I thought of the man in my dream and shut my eyes until the sound repeated itself. I was now awake enough to recognize it as knocking on my door.

"Queen Makeda?" Sarahil, my handmaiden, called out worriedly when I didn't immediately answer.

"It's okay. Come in," I told her.

Sarahil quietly entered and bent over to pick up my pillows. Her short dark hair was pulled into a tight knot, as was the apron around her plump waist.

"Sarahil, I don't understand why I keep dreaming about this man. Who is he?"

I'd known Sarahil since she was assigned to me at birth. She was twenty years older than I was, and I'd come to rely upon her wise advice. After all, growing up a princess hadn't afforded me opportunities to date or experiment with the opposite sex, even though I'd felt the natural curiosities of adolescence. And now that I was queen—following my father's death two years earlier—I would never have the chance to date or get married. You see, my country's customs and spiritual laws required me to remain an unwed virgin throughout my reign. "You are now and forever married to

Almaqah, the sun god," my priests had emphasized during my coronation.

As Sarahil bathed me in warm springwater mixed with oils and fragrant flowers, I remembered something from my dream. "He was wearing sandalwood oil," I said aloud.

"Who was wearing sandalwood, Queen Makeda?"

"The man in the dream, Sarahil! Oh, how I wish Mother was here! She knew the meaning and fortune behind every dream."

"Yes, well, your mother was of the magical kind. . . ."

"You can say the word, Sarahil. My mother was a Jinn."

"She never liked that name, Queen Makeda. She preferred the term *Genie*. She thought *Genie* sounded more regal and dignified, since most people think of Jinn as small mischief makers. And some even call them *evil!*"

"Well, most people don't realize that the Jinn are just one of the five types of Djinn. They get us Jinn all mixed up with the depraved Ghuls and Shaytan. Maybe Mom was right! We *do* need a different name for the Jinn, since we're the Djinn group that's always trying to do the right thing."

Sarahil rubbed extra oil onto my feet—as if the treatment would help my Jinn feet look normal—and lovingly scraped the furlike hair from my four toes. Yet no matter how much oil she poured onto them,

Sarahil still couldn't hide my misshapen feet, which betrayed my Jinn origins. They were great for climbing trees; walking barefoot down hot, rocky paths; and stamping out fires. Yet as the young queen of one of the largest commonwealths surrounding the Red Sea, I wanted normal, human five-toed feet more than anything.

Well, almost anything, I thought, recalling my dream. Sarahil's faraway stare told me that she was reminiscing about my mother, and her foot massage took my mind off the dream.

Sarahil's focus returned. "Time to get you dressed, Queen Makeda. Captain Tamrin is returning today, and he wants to give you the official report about his journey."

She slid my rings from the tail of my cat. Abby had the longest, skinniest tail of any of our palace cats and loved holding my rings for me while I bathed. Her large ears pointed skyward, and she looked at me and purred.

As Sarahil dried me with a thick fluffy towel, I fingered the red stone on a golden chain around my neck, a gift from my dying father that I never removed. Sarahil wrapped soft green beaded cotton fabric snugly around my chest and arms, the cloth swinging freely from the waist down. It was one of hundreds of gowns, colorfully and elaborately embroidered especially to flatter my brown skin and black hair. Each one was floor-length to cover my twisted Jinn toes.

I impatiently allowed Sarahil to rub perfumed unguent cream on my face to protect my now-seventeen-year-old skin from the harsh sun and dry air. Unguent was the one thing that kept desert women looking young and supple. But I couldn't sit still long enough for her to line my eyes with kohl.

"So, when will I see Tamrin and hear all about his latest adventures?" I asked anxiously. Tamrin's stories of leading our Royal Trade Caravan were always so entertaining. And his excursions were profitable, too, as Tamrin kept our coffers filled with gold and imported products. He traveled by ship and camel caravan to sell and barter our red gold, cedarwood, marble, frankincense, myrrh, and other rich resources throughout Africa and Asia.

"Right after breakfast," answered Sarahil as she led me to the dining table, where food was already laid out. I hurriedly scooped the fava-bean scramble onto my injera bread. I wiped my mouth and looked around for Sarahil. *Why did she always disappear when I was eating?*

I was two steps toward the garden courtyard door when Sarahil's arm slipped through mine. "Let me take a look at you," she said, turning my face toward hers. "Hmm, some wild-iris blend ought to bring those gorgeous lips of yours back to life." Sarahil dabbed her finger on the open vial she held in her hand and rubbed the substance on my lips.

"Ouch!" I pressed my fingers against my lips, hoping to stop the burning sting that compelled them to swell and grow darker.

"*Now* you're ready to meet him," Sarahil said authoritatively, as we walked to my favorite bench beneath the rose tree. I closed my eyes and inhaled, but instead of smelling roses, I detected sandalwood. Was I back in the dream . . . ?

"You didn't think I'd forgotten your birthday, my queen?" My musings were interrupted.

"Tamrin!" I hugged his neck in very unroyal fashion. Tamrin was like a favorite uncle who always brought me exotic presents and entertained me with endless stories. He lifted me up by the shoulders and twirled me around.

"Balkis!" he bellowed in his warm, affectionate way, using the pet name very few even knew, let alone called me by. Tamrin's distinctive voice had a deep baritone, musical quality about it. Every word he spoke moved up and down a cascading scale of notes. "Happy seventeenth, my queen!"

Before I even had a chance to admire it, Tamrin placed an emerald-encrusted gold-filigree necklace around my neck, above the chain from my father. I looked down to see that it pointed toward my bustline. Tamrin caught my stare and smiled. My body had definitely matured during his absence!

"Well, the good news is that we only lost one man and a few camels on this trip," he recounted, sitting next to me on the bench. Normally, I needed lots of space between myself and other people, but

Tamrin—well, with him it was different. In fact, since my parents' passing, Tamrin and Sarahil were the closest thing to family that I had.

"Where did you go?" I tucked my legs beneath me on the bench's silken pad and leaned forward to soak in every nuance of Tamrin's travel tales.

Tamrin smiled and, as usual, his eyes disappeared into his round red cheeks. His eyes always reminded me of twin crescent moons turned upside down.

"I've just returned from a land called Israel and their capital city of Jerusalem. The King of Israel purchased many of our goods and also sent gifts for you and our people."

As much as I wanted to hear about the gifts, I was more curious about Tamrin's journey. Since I'd never traveled, I was eager to experience it through his words.

"The trip was mostly treacherous, Queen Balkis. Nothing for a lady, that's for sure." Tamrin stroked his neatly trimmed beard, which had grown more gray since he'd left. His eyes sported more lines around them as well. Poor Tamrin. He so enjoyed traveling, but at what price to his own body and health?

Tamrin continued his description of the journey: "Nearly 1,500 miles of sand, wind, high seas, and occasional marauders. The ships handled the chop and swells, but the men and animals had to rest frequently, which slowed us down. We had allotted six months for the journey, but what with the monsoon season and the king wanting to host us for some time, we've been gone for over a year!"

A year! Had it really been that long since I'd listened to Tamrin's enthralling stories? No wonder I was starving to hear his tales.

"Please tell me about the king's hosting, Tamrin," I begged. It was customary for royalty to put dignitaries up as their guests. I'd do the same if the king's caravan were to ever visit our land.

"Ah, it was a lavish affair from day one! Every type of meal you could dream of, always served on golden trays by well-mannered servants who seemed genuinely happy with their work. The king loves music, song, poetry, and dance, so all our meals were accompanied by the height of entertainment. It was also entertaining to watch the king at work. Even at his age, he's already gained quite a reputation as a wise one." Tamrin leaned toward me and whispered, "They also say that the king has the gift of magic!"

I imagined a gray-bearded wizard sitting on his throne, dispensing magical spells and wise proclamations. "How old is he?" I asked.

"The king of Israel is relatively new to the post and very young, like you," Tamrin replied. "His father, King David, was a great man of legendary proportions. David became king not by inheritance, as you did, but by winning a contest and killing one of the giants."

I shuddered. Everyone was afraid of giants, who acted more like vicious wild animals than people. Someone had once told me they were the offspring of sinister beings called Watchers, coupling with mortal women. I wondered whether this was true.

Tamrin went on: "David was just a shepherd boy who bravely decided to help the Hebrews win their battle against the Philistines. He killed his giant with a rock flung from a slingshot. David instantly became a local hero, and the daughter of Israel's King Saul was among his many admirers. King Saul was jealous of David, so he gave him an impossible task to perform in exchange for his daughter's hand in marriage. David, ever the optimist, successfully completed it and became the king's son-in-law. David continued to act as a brave warrior, which increased both his popularity and the king's envy.

"King Saul decided to kill his rival, so David fled. He lived where he could, including among the Philistines, and even in a cave! He befriended the prophets, especially a famous one named Samuel, who declared that Israel's God wanted David to succeed Saul upon the throne. This enraged Saul even more, who stepped up his lethal pursuit of David. But Samuel's prophecy was clear: Saul would die in battle, and David would win his crown and throne.

"Sure enough, Saul found himself in an enormous battle where he was in mortal danger, so he ran for safety. Unfortunately, this decision made him more vulnerable, since he took flight without the protection of soldiers. Alone on the battlefield, Saul was killed. David's zealous fans helped to fulfill Samuel's prophecy and he became king."

I was sure there was more to the story, and I asked Tamrin to please continue.

"That's enough for today, Princess—I mean, *Queen*—Balkis." After two years, Tamrin still wasn't used to calling me by my new title. He patted my head and stood up. "I've got to attend to my men and the camels."

"Wait!" I pleaded, pulling on Tamrin's shirt as he walked away.

"I'll tell you more tomorrow morning," he promised before turning the corner out of the courtyard.

He was such a powerful man, with the ability to be blunt without offending me. I fingered the emerald necklace and walked over to my sleeping lioness, Orit, who purred as I pet her.

I went to bed early that night because it seemed like a good way to speed up time so that I could hear more of Tamrin's stories. Visions of the magical kingdom of Israel played in my mind. I imagined myself visiting there someday, even though I knew my protectors would never allow me to cross the border and go outside of Saba. "Too much is at stake!" they'd warn.

We were a wealthy nation, rich in precious metals, stones, spices, and oils. Our water basins were always full, thanks to our Wādī Dhana watercourse and the Mārib Dam, which irrigated our crops and provided drinking water for our families. Our farmers grew bountiful grains and vegetables upon the terraced slopes of our wet highlands. Fortunately, since we sat at the lower edges of the Red Sea, our country was too isolated for invaders, and we'd enjoyed 500 years of peace and prosperity.

As royalty, I had my every need met. I was bathed, fed, and dressed in the finest ways. I didn't have to pay or work for anything. Sure, I had to attend boring staff meetings, sign documents, and occasionally make diplomatic decisions, but basically I could do whatever I wanted, whenever I wanted. I should have felt grateful, and ecstatic about my good fortune, but I didn't. Something was missing from my life . . . but what?

CHAPTER 2

I searched for him in my dreams. Where was he? Wasn't it time for our nightly rendezvous? And then when it was nearly daybreak, I saw him. My heart leapt as I ran into his arms, pushing my face against his shoulder. <u>Hold me!</u> I implored. His embrace tightened and I felt safe, protected, and loved. I merged with his sandalwood warmth and slept soundly at last. . . .

Once again our embrace was interrupted by annoying noises. This time it wasn't Sarahil knocking, though. *"Oop! Oop! Oop!"* the sound wailed from outside. My cat, Abby, pounced on the open windowsill to investigate. Like many of the buildings in Saba, my window was an elaborately carved and painted opening in the *'ilb*-wood and gypsum-plaster wall. Since my palace sat in the arid lowlands, there was no need for protection against cold or wind.

"Sarahil!" I yelled.

She was instantly at my bedside. "Yes, ma'am?"

"Hear that sound?"

Right on cue, the *"Oop! Oop! Oop!"* continued. Sarahil walked to the window and bent to look outside. "Why, it's a beautiful bird, Queen Makeda."

"Oop! Oop! Oop!" The chirping was insistent. Abby hissed and issued warning gurgles at the bird.

I ran to the window to have a look. "I've never seen anything like him!" The bird's strawberry-blond head sported a crown topped with black tips, and his wings and tail were striped like a zebra.

"Why, he's beautiful!" I marveled as the bird spread his wings and perched on the tree above the garden courtyard.

Seeing the courtyard reminded me of my upcoming appointment to hear more about the kingdom of Israel. "When will Tamrin be here?" I asked.

"Right after breakfast," Sarahil replied, brushing my long black hair into a roll. She then pinned some white orchids beneath my gemstone-encrusted gold crown. I tucked my father's neck chain beneath my dress and wore my new emerald necklace to honor Tamrin (and, I admit, to encourage him to keep bringing me gifts!).

Tamrin was already seated waiting for me when I entered the courtyard after breakfast. So was the striped bird, who sat in the rose tree above the bench. *"Oop! Oop! Oop!"* he called.

"How remarkable," Tamrin said as we both stared. "That looks incredibly similar to a bird I kept seeing in Israel. I think they called it a hoopoe bird. It's supposed to be really smart and have magical abilities."

"Well, *I* think he's stupid," I huffed. "He's spying on our meeting, as well as keeping you from telling me more of your story!" Upon uttering those words, I could swear that the bird looked right at me and glared!

"Solomon would simply ask the bird what his motives were," Tamrin quipped.

"Who?"

"Solomon—King Solomon," Tamrin replied as if I should already know this information. "He's the king of Israel, the land from which I just returned."

Tamrin had led a merchant fleet of seventy-three ships, all filled with men, camels, and commodities. They'd sailed up the Red Sea and then disembarked to ride their camels to the royal palace, where King Solomon's men awaited. Tamrin had successfully sold them all of his merchandise, consisting of precious metals, silks, gemstones, and spices. The profits were sure to boost our already-wealthy economy.

"So why would a rich king talk to a hoopoe bird?" I wondered aloud.

"Ah, King Solomon is a complex man, filled with many mysteries. No wonder the ladies all desire him."

Tamrin looked straight into my eyes, trying to read my reaction to his words.

I remained purposely stoic, although inside I was definitely intrigued. "Hmm," I countered in my most neutral tone. In my head, though, I screamed for Tamrin to tell me more.

"Well, I can see that you're not really interested in hearing about this." Tamrin played my bluff and pretended to leave.

"Wait!" I laughed. "I *command* you to tell me more!"

Tamrin winked and continued: "King Solomon has built an enormous and elaborate temple to house his religion's sacred artifacts. Our country's red gold and gemstones were used in the construction of this holy place. In fact, the king has purchased items from merchants far and wide."

"It must be *some* temple!" I muttered, not wanting to interrupt Tamrin's flow of words.

"Oh, my dear Balkis," nodded Tamrin, "this is so much more than a temple. To understand it, I must first explain the background of this project."

I plumped two thick, round canvas pillows behind my back and settled in to hear the story.

Tamrin began: "A man named Moses once walked the lands from Egypt to Israel, leading slaves to freedom. Moses was attuned to the great Divine voice. By following its guidance, he was able to feed and protect his group during their long journey. The great Divine voice often materialized in miraculous ways, which included presenting Moses with two stone tablets etched with words."

"What did the words say?" I leaned closer.

"The great Divine voice provided Moses and his followers with a set of instructions that are now referred to as 'the Ten Commandments.' The etched tablets were miraculous because they were a materialization of the voice. Moses and his followers, even unto today, believe that there is one sole God, which they spell with a capital *G*. Their God is a male deity whom they call Adonai or Yahweh. He creates and controls everything. They believe that if they worship him and follow the Ten Commandments, he will protect and watch over them. Their God also sends beings to Earth called *angels* to deliver messages and guidance."

"One God! And only a *male* God?" I'd never heard of, or even considered, such a foreign concept. I'd always accepted that our pantheon of gods and goddesses was the single, unquestionable truth. And how could anyone deny that the sun, with its nurturing rays, was the giver of life? My head felt funny as I contemplated that there might be something more.

"Yes, they refer to him as 'the One True God of Israel,'" explained Tamrin. "Their beliefs are what's called *monotheistic,* which means 'having one God,' and their term for their religion is *Judaism.* Apparently, it extends back to another historical man named Abraham, whom they consider the patriarch or father of Judaism."

"Do you mean Brahma, the Indian Hindu god?" I asked.

"No," replied Tamrin, "although there are some similarities, besides the closeness in the spelling of their names. For instance, Brahma's wife was Sarasvati, and Abraham's was Sarah. But beyond that, Abraham's story involves discovering the One True God of Israel."

"So their God of Israel must be huge, if he's the only one involved in their lives." I chose my words carefully, not sure if this was an entirely proper thing to say. "No wonder the king has built a magnificent temple for him."

"Yes," agreed Tamrin. "They say that God himself gave the building plans to Solomon's father, King David. God was quite specific in the measurements for his temple."

"So why didn't David build the temple back then?"

"David had blood on his hands. His involvements in war and the killing of his lover's husband disqualified him from building the holy temple," said Tamrin. "The job was passed to his son, who showed great wisdom and integrity from an early age. Whereas David's legacy was a strong military force, which he used to

amass vast fortunes, allies, and land, Solomon's kingdom revels in prosperity, peacefulness, and the beauty
of architecture. Since his fourth year as king, Solomon's
focus has been building the temple. "

"So the temple is a place of worship, like our solar
temples?" I asked.

"Actually, it's the new residence for the Ark of the
Covenant," Tamrin answered. I swore that he enjoyed
talking in riddles.

"The Ark of the *what?*"

"It's an interesting story, but a long one." Tamrin
stood up and brushed his clothes and hair free of the
flower petals that had dropped from the vines hanging
from the courtyard's trellis.

"Wait, don't stop yet!" I pleaded, but Tamrin bowed
and began to back away.

I trailed after him, but as much as I begged Tamrin to have lunch with me so that I could continue
hearing the story, he declined. "I have a whole herd of
camels and many men to attend to. We've got to keep
Sheba's economy strong, Queen Balkis."

"But . . ." Tamrin smiled and sealed my protests
with a finger over my lips. He kissed the top of my
head, bowed again, and promised to return in the
morning for the story's next installment.

👑 👑 👑

CHAPTER 3

I was so engrossed in Tamrin's story that I hadn't noticed that the sun was nearly overhead—time to go to our afternoon worship service! I walked to the awaiting chariot and was grateful that Sarahil had brought my hat and fan, as the sun was even hotter than normal.

We raced along the path until we saw the tips of the Awam Temple's tall obelisks, like fingers of the sun extending upward to create the dawn. The sound of drumming, singing, and music told us that we were rapidly approaching the outdoor temple.

I jumped out of the carriage before it fully stopped within the temple's circular enclosure. Sarahil hurried behind me to meet the people who were already kneeling before the statues in front of each obelisk.

Two men rolled out my golden carpet so that I could kneel. Everyone had their own carpet, usually of the hand-knotted variety. Mine was placed on an elevated platform, and I sometimes felt self-conscious when the sun reflected from the gilded threads embroidered into my elaborate and oversized rug. These were the moments when I just wanted to be like everyone else. Still, custom called for royalty to be elevated above the populace, so I banished these thoughts quickly.

Our high priest led us through the service. As he named and said prayers to each of the eight members of our pantheon of sun, moon, and star deities, we all bowed in the direction of each statue and its symbols. Every southern Arabian commonwealth had its own primary deity, and ours was Almaqah, the sun god. In fact, Sabaeans (residents of Sheba) were often referred to as "the Children of Almaqah." We consulted him for guidance and protection in everything, but especially when it came to growing healthy and fertile crops.

Our secondary deity was Athtar, the god of the star Venus. He was in charge of creating rain, which was essential for our crops and for providing drinking water. Athtar had a temper, though, and sometimes he'd throw thunder and lightning to exhibit his displeasure with us, so we continually gave him offerings to entreat him to send rain without violent storms. Athtar's wife was Hawbas, the Venus goddess. Both deities were symbolized in our temple by eight-pointed stars, which represented Venus.

Our moon god's name was Ta'lab, and his symbol was the crescent, which we inscribed on many of our buildings and especially on his temple obelisk. Our pantheon also included Almaqah's daughters, the solar goddesses dhāt-Hinyan and dhāt-Ba'danum. We offered gilded statues and other gifts to the deities in exchange for their favors, protection, and guidance from their oracle, which was given through the priests.

One of Sheba's chief exports was incense, which we made from the frankincense and myrrh trees that flourished on our stony hillsides. Each springtime, workers would cut incisions in the trees and collect their oozing white gum, which was then shaped into small balls and dried into incense. We had incense burners *everywhere* in Sheba, and particularly at our temples. You could always smell the sweet and pungent fragrances day and night throughout the land.

During ceremonies, priests poured water into the drains of stone altars as a way of returning the gift of rain back to our beloved gods and goddesses. Then the high priest would point to the space between each obelisk, which he used to track the positions of the sun, moon, and stars. He gave a divination reading for our commonwealth based upon their movements while we all chanted prayers in unison.

I was enjoying the ceremony when suddenly the sky darkened. Startled, everyone looked overhead to see what might eclipse the great sun. Could it be a sign of the god's displeasure? A rainstorm? . . . No, it was a flock of birds, packed in so tightly that few sun rays could penetrate from above. I blinked at the lead bird because it looked like the hoopoe from the courtyard.

After a few awkward moments, the ceremony was resumed. A muscular young man wearing white draped pants and a tight-fitting shirt rhythmically beat a small drum called a *kebero*. He was joined by other young men shaking handheld rattles, known as *sistrums,* while a tall figure played a long *khallol* flute accompanied by a *masenqo* fiddler.

Five young women swayed in unison to the music. A tall woman in the middle spun around so that her sheer green skirt swung outward in a circle. She lifted her scarf veil to the sky and waved it repeatedly around her head. The effect was beautiful, and I clapped in appreciation.

"I want to try dancing like that," I told Sarahil.

"But Queen Makeda, you know that royalty aren't allowed to dance," she countered.

"Why not?" I protested. I walked over to the tall dancer. "Can you show me how to do that?"

The woman appeared embarrassed, unsure how to handle the situation. "It's all right." I touched her shoulder reassuringly. The dancer looked at Sarahil, who reluctantly nodded.

The woman gulped and wordlessly motioned for me to mimic her movements. Her hips undulated in a figure-eight motion, both horizontally and vertically.

I tried to coax my hips to move like hers: down, then right, then up, then left—but my muscles felt stuck in one place.

The dancer motioned to her heart and said, "Think from here. Your body knows what to do."

Think from my heart. Hmm, I wasn't sure how to do that, but I was willing to give it a try if it meant I could look like her.

"Please take this," she said, handing me her scarf veil. I swung it over my head as she had done, but instead of flying gracefully, the scarf became entangled in my crown! I looked over at Sarahil and the others, who were politely suppressing their laughter.

"From here," the dancer repeated, patting my heart. She indicated for me to hold the veil behind my head and rock back and forth, which was easy enough to do. "Close your eyes and sway to the music," she instructed.

The dancer and Sarahil faded away, and I found myself moving around a circle of rocks with other women. We were beautiful free spirits flexing and bending gracefully around one another. I wore a sheer skirt that was too short to cover my feet, but I didn't care because the other women's feet looked exactly like mine. And for once, I thought that my feet looked beautiful!

One of the women seemed so familiar as she danced toward me. "Mother!" I yelled, running over to her excitedly. Tears streamed down my cheeks, and my heart leapt with joy . . . I'd missed her so much. "Mother! Over here! It's me, Makeda!"

But she looked right through me as if I weren't there and just kept dancing. I collapsed on one of the rocks and cried out for my mother. . . .

"Are you okay, Queen Makeda?"

My mother and the other women disappeared, and I was back at the temple. The dancer and Sarahil stood over me, looking concerned.

"What's wrong?" Sarahil inquired as she put her hand on my forehead to check if I was overheated.

I handed the veil back to the dancer and asked Sarahil and the chariot driver to return me immediately to the palace.

Once we arrived, I rushed into my bedroom wordlessly and pushed my face into my pillow. Years of pent-up grief and anger burst to the surface. I silenced my sobs with the pillow so that Sarahil wouldn't worry.

Why did everyone have to die? First my beautiful mother, so magical and carefree—no wonder she'd attracted the romantic attention of a king! Actually, my father had *become* king because of my mother's help. He'd told me the story often:

A fierce dragon held our commonwealth in terror by stealing young maidens from their families. No traces of these women were ever recovered, so everyone assumed the worst about their fate. The elderly and ailing king of Saba was powerless to stop the dragon's murderous trail.

The warriors of the land searched everywhere for the dragon's lair—without success—so the king issued a decree that whoever slew the dragon would inherit his throne and crown.

Soon after, my father was in the forest when a beautiful gazelle stopped and looked at him. My father swore that he heard the animal's wry voice asking him to follow.

The gazelle led my father along riverbeds and up and down mountains. The gentle doe stopped whenever my father needed to rest. When they reached the bottom of a rocky valley, the gazelle stood at attention. Even her ears, tail, and fur were raised; and her body twitched nervously. She looked at my father and directed his gaze to the entrance of a cave.

My father heard rumbling sounds inside the cave, and his gut tightened. The gazelle had led him to the murderous dragon's lair! He looked at his sword and knew it was inadequate to penetrate the dragon's thick hide. What should he do?

The gazelle swung her right leg back and forth, lifting dirt and leaves with each swing. Her actions seemed deliberate, so my father walked over to investigate. He picked up some leaves and discovered a hole underneath filled with rocks! He immediately understood the gazelle's message and began removing the stones from the hole. As soon as he'd created a space large enough for himself, my father wiggled into it. The gazelle used her horns and hooves to cover my father's head with leaves and then walked to the mouth of the lair.

My father could hear the gazelle pounding her hooves against the rocky entrance and uttering bark-like sounds. He felt nervous as he realized that the gazelle seemed to be baiting the dragon, trying to attract its attention. A loud rumbling sound proved his theory correct!

There was nothing subtle about the dragon's movements, and my father was able to track its every step. Fortunately, the gazelle could outrun any animal, especially slow-footed wingless dragons. The smell of burning leaves told my father that the dragon had snorted an angry fit of fire. My father was poised, ready with his sword pointing upward.

The gazelle treaded lightly across the leaves covering my father, and the dragon followed. Fortunately, the surrounding rocks prevented the dragon from falling on top of him. He momentarily considered piercing the dragon's vulnerable underbelly, but he hesitated too long and the opportunity passed.

The pace of the dragon's footsteps picked up, and my father peered through the leaves to see a thin young woman in a gauze dress standing near the ledge of the mountain. There was no sign of the gazelle. My father scrambled out of the rocky hole to save her (he didn't exactly know how he'd do this, but his intentions were noble).

The woman stood her ground at the mountain's edge as the dragon galloped toward its prey. She didn't scream or even blink.

What happened next was something my father only admitted to my mother and me after years of our begging for the full story:

The woman jumped from the ledge into a bush, and a gazelle, frightened by the commotion, scurried away. My father recognized the gazelle by her distinctive markings as the one who'd led him to the lair. The dragon, unable to stop its course, careened straight off the mountain and fell to its death.

"You killed the dragon!" a chorus of men's voices chimed in, as my father turned around to see who had witnessed the event.

One of the men knelt before him. "Long live the new king!" The others joined in the chant and lifted my father onto their shoulders.

My father and the men hiked to the bottom of the ravine, where the dragon lay lifeless. My father said, "Sorry, big fellow. If only you'd had an appetite for something other than young maidens and gazelles!" He then blessed the animal's soul and ceremoniously cut out its heart to undo the dark spell that the dragon had cast over Sheba. He skillfully used his sword to extract the magical blood-red stone contained within every dragon's heart.

On his way back, my father searched everywhere for the beautiful young woman who'd narrowly escaped death . . . and finally, he found her. She smiled and walked up the pathway, with my father following close behind. No matter how many questions he asked, though, the woman had the same reply: a silent smile. By the time they reached my father's home, he was smitten. That evening, under the full moon, my father proposed marriage to her.

The whole commonwealth of Saba was ecstatic: Not only was the dragon slain (the unmistakable dragon stone that my father presented to the royal advisors proved this), but the new king was a fair, kind, and wise man. The commonwealth held a weeklong ceremony in honor of my parents' marriage, followed by my father's coronation.

Several years after their wedding, my father pressed my mother for details about her fall from the mountain as the dragon had charged her. After some prodding, my mother confessed the truth about

her Jinn heritage and how she'd shape-shifted into a
gazelle to help my father that day. Fortunately, this
made him love her even more!

I fingered the long golden chain that my father
had handed me while he lay dying. "This will protect
you and help you to be brave," he'd said. I held up the
beveled blood-red stone at the end of the chain and
admired its various colors and nuances. It was hard to
believe that something so beautiful had been inside a
dragon's heart!

My memories of my mother were sketchier. Mostly
I remembered her frequent unexplained absences. I
eventually learned that Mother came from the magical
clan of the Jinn—petite people who live outdoors in
the forest and work closely with the elemental forces
of the world, such as fire, earth, and even the wind.
They can shape-shift into any appearance that suits
their purpose. That's why my mother chose to appear
as a gazelle to my father when they first met.

I looked down at my feet and shuddered at the one
reminder of my Jinn heritage. Why couldn't I have
inherited the ability to shape-shift or invoke wondrous
magic?

CHAPTER 4

"Why, you're already up!" Sarahil exclaimed. She usually had to wake me for my bath and breakfast, but I hadn't let myself sleep late for once. After crying myself to sleep the night before, I felt relatively cheerful this morning: Today I'd hear more about Tamrin's journey to Israel!

When I arrived in the courtyard, Tamrin was already waiting for me, watching flamingos gracefully bathe in the pond. Overhead in the trailing jasmine vines, the hoopoe bird cooed away. I decided to ignore him and not give him the satisfaction of annoying me. Instead, I pushed aside some pillows and removed my shoes. I didn't mind if Tamrin saw my feet. He once remarked that they were a sign of beauty, since the Jinn were such lovely people. Maybe someday I'd come to regard them as beautiful, too.

Tamrin must have caught me staring downward, because he coughed to get my attention. "The Ark of the Covenant," he began, picking up right where we'd left off the day before, "is a wooden box with an overlay of gold containing the two stone tablets that the Israeli God gave to Moses, as well as other sacred items such as a rod belonging to Moses's brother that provided miraculous protection as the two were escaping from Egypt.

"Up until recently, the Ark had been carried by Israelites as they traveled about. When Jerusalem became the center of Judaic life, an elaborate tent was erected. Called the Tabernacle, it housed the Ark for all these years, until the Ark was moved into the temple, which is now completed except for a few minor architectural touches."

"Was the tent secure enough for such a valuable and historical item?" I asked. Even though our country was relatively free of theft, I'd heard of temples being ransacked for their valuables.

"The Ark of the Covenant is its own protection," Tamrin answered cryptically. "It emits a power that, like the mighty sun, burns those who get too close to it. Only the highest and purest of priests and priestesses can approach the Ark. Even then, *any* egoic thoughts, actions, or words can set off dangerous effects."

"Dangerous! How so?" I couldn't imagine how a box of sacred objects could pose a threat.

"The energy of the Ark radiates so strongly that you must be in a state of inner peace to get near it. Anyone holding selfish or impure motives is out of sync with the Ark's energy. Such misalignment can be fatal!"

This still didn't make sense to me, so Tamrin continued his explanation: "The Ark is kept within a temple room called the Holy of Holies. Prior to visiting the Ark, the high priests and priestesses have silken ropes tied to their ankles. That way, if they should die during the visitation, their bodies can be pulled out without endangering their rescuers."

"So only the high priests and high priestesses ever see the Ark?" I asked. I secretly hoped that *I* could someday gaze upon the Ark of the Covenant.

"King Solomon is the exception, but otherwise, yes, that's correct."

"You mean the king is *so* pure that he can approach the holy Ark?"

Tamrin inhaled deeply. His exhalation was slow and deliberate. "King Solomon is . . ." Tamrin rubbed his chin and studied the ground. "King Solomon is undoubtedly . . ." He looked up.

"What, Tamrin? He's what?!" I bounced up and down in anticipation.

"Balkis, I can't find the words to describe him," Tamrin said finally.

I decided to help: "Is he bright and intelligent?"

"He's the wisest man anyone has ever met," Tamrin replied. "Since he was a young boy, King Solomon has settled disputes with wisdom."

"Is he articulate?"

"His words flow like golden honey, and everyone who hears him is transfixed."

"Is he physically fit and attractive?"

"Only the statues of Grecian gods are in better physical condition and more attractive than King Solomon."

"Surely he must have *some* human flaws," I quipped.

"Well, this is just a personal observation from my brief meetings with him." Tamrin looked around and whispered, "There was something in his eyes that looked lonely. I thought it was really ironic—after all, he's one of the most powerful and 'perfect' men in the world. He has everything, including the constant attention of servants, dignitaries, and admirers. Yet his eyes looked hollow, as if they were missing something important."

Just like I've been feeling! I said to myself—I didn't dare let Tamrin think that I was ungrateful for all that he, Sarahil, and everyone did.

CHAPTER 5

Once again, I was in his arms. He explored my back with his hands in a way that was both relaxing and exciting. As he tickled my cheeks with his beard, we both laughed: "<u>Oop! Oop! Oop!</u>" The laughter grew louder, and his grasp broke away from me. I reached for him, but he faded out of view as the sound intensified. . . .

Abby leapt from my bed to the windowsill. I pulled my blankets over my head and groaned. The hoopoe bird was back, after five mornings of blissful quiet. I half considered sending one of my guards to arrest the bird, who seemed completely undisturbed by Abby's presence!

Sarahil stuck her head out the window to shoo the bird away. "He's got something in his beak, ma'am."

She flinched and took a step backward as the bird flew onto the windowsill and dropped the item into my room. It certainly looked like he did it deliberately!

I wanted to sleep some more and return to my delicious dream, but curiosity got the best of me, so I threw off my bedcovers and rushed over to the item before Sarahil even had a chance to bend to pick it up.

"It's a scroll!" I exclaimed as I opened it. "With funny markings on it."

Sarahil peered over my shoulder and said, "Definitely another language. It looks familiar, but I surely can't read it." Although Saba was a highly literate commonwealth, and she and I both knew how to read, the markings were in a foreign script.

We both looked at each other and screamed in unison: "Tamrin!"

Sarahil rushed through my bath and hurriedly dressed me. Clutching the scroll with my left hand, I grabbed some injera bread from the table and hurried to the courtyard. I hoped that Tamrin would arrive earlier than usual to relieve me of the suspense.

I fingered the scroll. It was dark and surprisingly large, considering the fact that the bird had flown with it. I held it to my forehead and felt tingling sensations. A pungent fragrance enveloped me. I smelled the scroll directly: *What was that familiar scent?*

"Are you a messenger now?" Tamrin laughed heartily, his eyes disappearing into his red cheeks. I never tired of this phenomenon!

"No such luck! I'm stuck being queen." I giggled, handing the scroll to Tamrin.

The paper creaked as he unrolled it. His eyes and cheeks darkened. "It's from King Solomon," he said, scooting me to the right so that he could sit next to me on the bench.

"What does it say?" I demanded to know.

Tamrin mopped his forehead with his shirtsleeve and mumbled something that I couldn't understand— I had the feeling I shouldn't press him for information. Finally Tamrin spoke: "He's inviting you to his royal palace."

I looked at Tamrin, not needing to vocalize all my questions.

"The king . . ." he muttered, moving his foot around in the dust and sand that had fallen out of the scroll. I didn't blink or breathe as I waited. That's when I noticed the hoopoe bird's absence—he and his noise had been our daily companion in the courtyard for the last two weeks. Finally Tamrin spoke: "King Solomon, the one I was telling you about. He wants you to visit him, and he's issued an official invitation."

My heart fluttered and I swallowed hard. The sky darkened and I felt dizzy. I hadn't traveled anywhere significant in my entire life! Was it even possible for me to leave Saba? My stomach felt strange, and the bushes surrounding the courtyard seemed to spin in circles around me. I even thought I saw my mother's face peering out of one of them.

Tamrin looked directly at me. The seriousness and intensity of his gaze unsettled me. "We'll have to talk with the High Council," he said at last. "I'll call a meeting."

I wanted this moment to last forever, with Tamrin beside me in the chariot on our way to the temple that afternoon. I felt so close to him, even closer than I did to Sarahil (*would she ever forgive me if she knew I was thinking that?*). Tamrin's presence made me feel safe. I trusted the wisdom of his decisions. He squinted and gave me a sideways smile as I hugged him.

"Now, what's that for, Queen Balkis?" He laughed, but always kept one eye on the road: Tamrin was a true caravan leader.

"Tamrin, let's travel to Jerusalem together, okay?"

"Maybe," he chuckled. "Maybe."

The moon and stars were shining brightly by the time the High Council could meet with Tamrin and me. As I walked toward the room, I sensed tension and anger. I opened the door to hear Tamrin and my council of royal advisors in a heated discussion.

I peered into the room before entering. Kabede, a tall, elderly man who'd worked with my father and served as our chief high priest, held the scroll while the others looked over his shoulder to read it. Kabede pointed to one section and huffed, "This is completely unacceptable! I will not hear of it!"

I padded softly into the room to avoid interrupting his words. I needn't have worried, as everyone was completely focused on the scroll.

"How *dare* he speak to us—and especially to our queen—in this manner!" barked Kabede.

Tamrin shook his head, gulped down a tankard of wine, and grumbled, "He's gobbling up all of the nearby kingdoms to build his Israeli empire, and now he's demanding that the commonwealth of Sheba kneel before him as well!"

Kabede handed the scroll to another advisor, who added, "Apparently it's not enough for King Solomon to use all of our red gold for his palace and temple projects. He wants the rest of our land, too!"

I was grateful that I'd learned from my cat, Abby, how to enter rooms silently. Finally, Tamrin noticed me sitting in a soft padded chair near the conference table.

"Why, Queen Balkis!" Tamrin's eyes *also* disappeared in his cheeks when he was angry. The council members all bowed quickly, eager to get back to the business at hand.

I put my hand up to signal that I was open to hearing the discussion. Why did everyone feel that they had to shield me from bad news? I'd always considered myself to be strong and open-minded . . . maybe others didn't see me that way.

Kabede didn't skip a beat. "I have half a mind to assemble an army and show him what we think of his invitation!" His words alarmed me. After all, the commonwealth of Saba hadn't needed a military force for 500 years.

"Now, gentlemen, gentlemen!" Tamrin stood up and waved his hands to quiet the room. His eyes met mine. "And Queen Balkis," he added.

I stood next to Tamrin and Kabede and asked them to read the scroll to me. They resisted doing so, until I finally declared, "The scroll was sent to me, so it's only right that I know what it says!"

Tamrin coughed and turned to the other council members, who all nodded in agreement. They knew that I was right!

Tamrin and I sat while Kabede stood and read the scroll:

> From me, King Solomon, who sends greetings and peace to you, Queen of Sheba, and to your nobles! You are no doubt aware that the Lord of the Universe has appointed me king over the beasts in the field, the birds in the air, the Shaytan, spirits, and ghosts.
>
> All of the kings of the east, west, north, and south are visiting my kingdom to greet and pay

homage to me. Now if you will come and do the same, I will honor you more than I've honored all the other royalty who have, and are, in attendance.

However, if you refuse my invitation to salute and pay homage to me, I will send out against you kings, legions, and riders. You might ask, "Who are these kings, legions, and riders?" The beasts in the field are my kings; the birds of the air are my riders; and the spirits, Shaytan, and ghosts are my legions. They will throttle you in your beds, slay you in the fields, and consume your flesh.

My jaw clenched and my heart thumped in my forehead as the words rang in my ears. What rude arrogance to demand that I pay homage to him or face torturous death! How vile of him to challenge me and threaten to send one of my own—the Djinn race known as Shaytan—to harm me! A simple invitation would have elicited my attention!

I'd been insulted and had to take action. But what would be my best course to teach this barbarian dictator a lesson?

"I'll go to Jerusalem," I pronounced so loudly that everyone's eyes, including my own, grew wider. "And I'll meet this King Solomon. Not because he's threatened me, but because I'm the ruler of a peaceful commonwealth. I'll teach King Solomon that power comes from civility, not from force!"

At first the council members' expressions seemed to applaud my boldness, but this was quickly followed by worry lines and hand-wringing. "Queen, let *us* go on your behalf!" they begged.

But my mind was made up. I raised my hand and said, "It's no longer a matter of whether I'll go, but *when*—which I'll need your help in deciding." I then left the room before I could see Tamrin's face, since he had the power to weaken my resolve.

The temperature of the palace hallway was always a mix of hot and cold, which tonight mirrored my own vacillating feelings. Finally, I reached my room, where Sarahil had already turned down my bed and lit my nightstand candle. *Sarahil* . . . I wondered whether she'd accompany me to Jerusalem.

As I blew out the candle, I imagined confronting the arrogant King Solomon. I'd show him what real power consisted of!

I must have slept that night, although I don't remember doing so. Mostly I lay on my right side, seething with anger, then I turned onto my left side while second-guessing my planned journey to Jerusalem.

My pillows and bedcovers were everywhere when Sarahil woke me the next morning. She didn't need to say anything—her eyes said it all.

"The answer is *yes*," she announced.

I rubbed my eyes.

"Of course I'll accompany you to Jerusalem."

"Sarahil, you understand that it's several months' journey through the hot and unforgiving desert? Even if weather conditions permit us to sail part of the way up the Red Sea, we're likely to encounter monsoons, marauders, or worse!"

"My place is by your side, my queen." Sarahil bowed in a solemn, almost grim way, as if foreshadowing tragedy.

No! I bit my lip to control my thoughts and keep them positive. Abby jumped onto my lap, sensing my need for comfort. I absentmindedly stroked her back all the way to the tip of her long tail, soothed by her purrs, which reverberated in my stomach. *Could Abby come with me?* I momentarily considered. My tears surprised me, and I wiped them away so that Sarahil wouldn't know about my mixed feelings.

While I ate breakfast, Sarahil directed a crew who packed my clothes and supplies for our journey. Everyone seemed extra quiet, as if they were holding their breath.

CHAPTER 6

Tamrin wanted to start our journey before daybreak. "The first day sets the tone for the entire trip," he said as he helped me climb into my palanquin, which consisted of a silken square mattress atop a wooden frame. The roof and mosquito-netting curtains shielded me from the sun and bugs, as well as offering me privacy.

Normally, I rode in a chariot pulled by two camels, but Tamrin explained that the wheels couldn't withstand the rough terrain between Saba and Israel. So I was perched in the equivalent of a portable bedroom. Long poles on the right and left sides of the palanquin were supported by a camel in front of me and another behind me.

"Saja is our best camel, Queen Balkis." Tamrin patted the large camel, which carried the two front poles of my palanquin. "She's a smooth strider and very easygoing. Behind you is Rukan, a strong one known for her endurance and lack of complaints."

I felt grateful for the camels' willingness to carry me across the desert to Jerusalem. Saja and Rukan were in good company: Our caravan of nearly 800 camels and donkeys were all laden with men, supplies, and gifts for King Solomon. Sarahil and I were among the only females in the group.

Tamrin lifted his right arm ceremoniously, and he proclaimed, "*Nahaba!* Travel swiftly!" loudly while dropping his arm to signal the beginning of our journey. Saja and Rukan walked tentatively, accustoming themselves to the weight of the palanquin.

Their smooth gait rocked me gently, and I realized how tired I was. I'd barely slept the night before due to my excitement over this trip. A part of me felt guilt over riding in my luxurious palanquin when Sarahil, Tamrin, and all the others were exposed to the elements, but then tiredness took over, and I lay back on the mattress and pillows and slept hard.

After riding more than twenty miles toward the Red Sea, we settled in for the night against a mountainous dune, which protected us from the winds. As I climbed down from my perch, it took a moment to get control of my legs. The wavelike motion of the camels' walk had affected my equilibrium!

The nighttime temperature had dropped, so I arranged my shawl over my neck. But then I forgot about my physical comfort as I caught sight of the stars overhead. Why were they so bright? Perhaps it was a positive omen for our journey.

Ta'lab, Athtar, and Hawbas, please guide us through this journey, I said silently to the nighttime deities. A star shot across the deep blue backdrop, as if to confirm that my prayer had been heard.

"Makeda!" said a quiet voice originating behind me. Instead of turning to see who'd called my name, I felt that my instincts commanded me to stand still. I controlled my breath and slowed it down. "Makeda!" the voice called again. It was definitely a woman's, probably Sarahil looking for me.

Another star shot across the night sky, and my eyes followed its trail to the side of the mountain dune where a shrub was moving. At first, I assumed the wind was wiggling it, until I caught sight of something moving inside its branches. I drew closer to investigate what type of animal would be active at night.

As I neared the shrub, I heard my name called again against a background of beautiful music. I looked down to see a circle of rocks, each one about the size of my hand, in front of the shrubbery. I suddenly felt tired, so I sat down inside the circle. I could hear Sarahil calling my name back at the campground. . . .

The campground and dune disappeared, and it was daytime. I sat in a circle of rocks, and the

*endless desert sand was replaced by luscious fra-
grant flowers, bright green vines, and vividly colored birds. I breathed in the sweet aroma of the
flowers and relaxed more deeply than I had in a
long while. I realized how stressed I'd been, with
my strange recurring dreams, Tamrin's homecom-
ing, the scroll from King Solomon, and now this
journey away from Saba. I was tired, and I lay
down to sleep.*

*"Makeda," a woman said, stroking my hair
lovingly. "It's me."*

*"Mother!" I threw my arms around her neck
as tears streamed down my cheeks. I pulled her
down to lie beside me. "I've missed you so much!"
I sobbed uncontrollably.*

*Mother held me tightly and rocked me gen-
tly. I hadn't felt so safe and loved since she'd left
this world. I wanted to ask her so many questions
about my life, why she'd died when Jinn had the
option of immortality, and how to handle my royal
functions. But I couldn't spoil the moment, so I
just breathed. It was enough to be with my mother
again.*

"Queen Makeda!" Sarahil's voice pierced through
my bliss, and I looked up to see her and Tamrin standing above me. I looked back over to Mother and was
horrified as she faded into the night sky. Tamrin

reached out to help me stand up, mumbling, "You're tired. Let's go."

Sarahil and Tamrin led me to my tent, which was large enough for five or six people. The extra space would go to waste, however, since I was the queen and would sleep alone, with armed guards stationed outside all night.

I cried myself to sleep. This was the second time I'd seen a mirage of my mother, and each time the experience reopened old wounds that I wanted to remain closed. I'd just reconciled myself to her absence and learned how to live without her. Mother and I had been so close, bonding over everything: our identical Jinn feet; our shyness and sensitivity; our reluctance to engage in royal pomp and circumstance; and our love of good, rich food. I pulled my satin comforter tightly around my shoulders, pretending it was Mother's embrace.

CHAPTER 7

The desert warmed up only moments after a spectacular display of colors announced the sun's arrival the next morning. Lizards slid sleepily out of their burrows to explore their meal options. *Our* camp breakfast was well under way, and I ate more than normal to soothe my still-stirred emotions. Besides, yesterday we'd stopped only long enough to perform our prayers and invocations and had skipped lunch entirely to ensure that we made good time on our journey. Who knew when I'd eat next?

It turned out that I was right to get full when I could, as our next meal was dinner. Tamrin and Sarahil seemed to watch me even more closely to ensure I wouldn't wander again into the nighttime desert. I snuggled next to them both by the campfire. "Tell me more about King Solomon," I pleaded to Tamrin. "What was his mother like?"

"Ahh, well, that's quite the story," replied Tamrin, moving his legs to get comfortable. One reason why Tamrin was such a good storyteller was that he enjoyed this role so much.

"Solomon's father, King David, noticed a beautiful woman bathing on her rooftop. The more he watched her, the more he was filled with overwhelming desire. So he sent a message for the woman to visit him at his palace. Her name was Bathsheba."

"That sounds like *Sheba!*" I remarked.

"You're right," Tamrin considered momentarily before continuing. "Well, Bathsheba and David had an irresistible chemistry and attraction for one another. Within moments of meeting, they were locked in a passionate embrace, like two soul mates reuniting across lifetimes. Their passion continued into David's royal bedroom, and Bathsheba was impregnated that night."

"So did they get married and raise Solomon, then?" I asked.

Tamrin looked down. "Well, it was a little more complicated than that. Bathsheba already had a husband named Uriah who was a member of David's military forces. David couldn't bear the thought of Bathsheba being with another man, and he wanted to raise their child with her. So he devised a very dark plan to make Bathsheba his own."

"What did he do?" Sarahil asked anxiously.

"David arranged for Uriah to serve on the front combat line on a dangerous mission. And sure enough, Uriah was killed. Although David hadn't murdered him with his own hands, he was still technically responsible for his death. When Bathsheba and David's son died soon after childbirth, they felt certain it was God's punishment for Uriah's death. Fortunately, though, the couple was able to stay together during all of this stress, and Bathsheba soon became pregnant again."

"With Solomon?" I asked, eager to hear about the man we were spending so much time journeying to meet. Then I recalled the king's rude "ultimatum" of an invitation, and I wondered how I would contain my annoyance upon meeting him.

Tamrin nodded. "Yes, their next son they called Solomon, which means 'peace,' and as a child he lived up to his name. From an early age, Solomon was different from King David's other sons. He didn't play with toy swords or engage in power struggles as his brothers did. He only wanted to read, and engage in philosophical discussions with adults. Like his father, Solomon had a clear connection to the Divine. He could hear the God of Israel very loudly.

"Legends say that God gave young Solomon the option of having anything he desired, such as wealth, power, or popularity. But Solomon told God that all he wanted was wisdom. God was so pleased with Solomon's answer that he gave him wisdom—plus wealth; power;

popularity; reign over all the people, animals, birds, and demons; and anything else that he wished for."

"How does he use his wisdom?" I inquired.

"Since he was a small boy, Solomon has held court to decide upon the legal, ethical, and moral matters his citizens bring him. His decisions are brilliant, which is one reason why travelers are attracted to Jerusalem.

"In fact," Tamrin continued, "as a youth, Solomon once settled a lawsuit between two boys! The dispute started when one boy was hungry and asked to borrow some of the other boy's breakfast. The second boy agreed to lend him one of his boiled eggs, under the condition that someday the first boy would have to repay it. Plus, the borrower would have to give money to the lender, to compensate for any profits that he might have made had he kept the egg."

"This is complicated," I commented.

"Years after the hungry boy had eaten the borrowed boiled egg, the second boy came to collect on the deal. He demanded an egg, which the first boy dutifully produced. Then the lending boy demanded a huge sum of money as repayment for the income lost from the time the egg was out of his possession. The two squabbled over this condition, so they finally agreed to ask King Solomon's father—King David—to settle the dispute."

"What did King David decide?" I asked.

"Well, David figured that the original egg would have produced many chickens over the years, so the large amount of money was rightfully due to the lending boy. On the way out of the courtroom, young Solomon talked with the boys about the situation. He advised the one who owed the large sum of money to stand in a farmer's field near the palace and drop boiled beans onto the tilled soil. 'Tell everyone you meet that you're planting boiled beans to grow crops,' Solomon counseled.

"The boy did this and soon grew a reputation as a crazy youth, since everyone knew that boiled beans couldn't produce crops. Word reached King David, who realized his error in judgment in citing that a boiled egg would have yielded profits and chickens for the lending boy. The lawsuit was dismissed, and David hailed his son as a wise and fair judge. From then on, Solomon was invited to participate in his father's court's proceedings.

"Solomon's dealings with legal cases are nothing short of genius!" Tamrin's eyes disappeared into his cheeks as he recalled a recent case:

> Three men traveling together by foot had a large number of coins, which they hid in the corner of an inn where they stayed on their way to their destination. When it was time to leave, the bag of coins had disappeared. The men accused each other of stealing the money, and since no one confessed or returned the coins, they took their situation to King Solomon's court.

After the king had heard the three men's stories, he decided to tell them an allegory, which would help Solomon to pinpoint the thief among them. He explained that a young boy and girl vowed to wed one another when they matured to marriageable ages. They also agreed that if either wanted to marry a different person, this would be okay if they first sought permission from each other.

Well, the girl grew older and fell in love with a different man, so she approached her childhood friend and asked for his permission to marry someone else. She even offered to give him a dowry settlement to release her from their agreement. But he refused the money and agreed immediately to her marriage.

On her way home, the young woman was robbed of the dowry money and the thief threatened to harm her. She cried to him for mercy and complained that the money had been refused by the young man she'd just visited. She said, "You should be ashamed that a man much younger than yourself refused to take my money. Someone your age should know better." Her words touched the thief's heart. He returned her money, and she reached home unharmed.

After Solomon had relayed this story to the three men in his courtroom, he asked them who in the story was most worthy of praise: the young

woman who kept her promise by asking permission to marry, the young man who readily gave his assent without accepting a financial bribe, or the thief who returned the money to the young woman?

The first man exclaimed that the young woman was the most praiseworthy, and the second man cited the young man as most heroic in the story. The third man then explained that the thief was the most admirable for returning the stolen money.

At that point, Solomon knew that the third man had stolen the bag of coins from his two friends, since he admired a thief. The third man admitted his guilt and returned the money.

I was genuinely impressed by Tamrin's report of Solomon's wisdom. As I fell asleep, I wondered what Solomon would talk about with *me*. Although I considered myself intelligent and well read, I worried whether I could hold engaging conversations with the wise king. My knowledge of the Hebrew language was minimal, so I was already at a social disadvantage.

The sun glared overhead as our caravan paralleled the Red Sea's coastline on our journey northward. Members of our party wore *shemagh*—protective cloths—wrapped around their heads, necks, and shoulders to shield them from the sun's hot rays. I silently prayed to Almaqah, the sun god, for relief. I was only a bit surprised when a small cloud appeared and drifted in front of the sun. After all, Almaqah was supposedly my husband, so of course he'd protect and rescue me from the heat!

I thought about Tamrin's story of King Solomon's legendary wisdom. *Was he really that wise?* I wondered. Instead of worrying about our compatibility, I decided to pray about this situation: "Almaqah, please help me to have interesting and intelligent discussions with King Solomon."

I immediately saw an image of Mother's face in my mind's eye and heard the word *riddles* in my right ear. *Riddles? What did that mean?* I wondered. I meditated on this word to the rhythm of my camels' rolling pace. I lay down and closed my curtains to darken the palanquin's interior.

Soon I was gone and dreaming of him. I hadn't seen his face since we'd begun the journey, so I ran excitedly into his arms. I inhaled his sandalwood scent and melted into his warm, muscular embrace.

He held my head and looked into my eyes. "I've missed you so much, my darling," he murmured as he nuzzled my face with his nose and chin.

His tenderness quickened my breath and heart. "Where have you been?" I inquired.

"Makeda! *No!*" a female voice interrupted. I turned to see my mother extending her arms toward me.

"Mother, what are you doing here?" I demanded to know.

"Saving you from a huge mistake!" she replied with tense firmness.

I sat stunned, my head buzzing with anger. I realized that I was now fully awake in my palanquin, and Mother was actually with me in the flesh. I touched her arm, then my own, just to double-check that I wasn't still dreaming. I momentarily forgot my anger over Mother's interruption and began to cry. I'd missed her so much!

Mother held me tightly while I sobbed like a little child. She gave me water to drink, and I breathed deeply.

"Mother?" I spoke through my tears. I wanted to ask her why she'd left me. Why was she here now? Was I imagining her? Was I seeing her apparition from the spirit world?

But Mother put her finger to my lips to silence my questions. "I'll tell you everything, my sweet daughter," she promised. I reclined into her gentle embrace and fell back asleep.

❧

Tamrin's voice outside woke me up, and I remembered Mother. I opened my eyes, expecting her to be gone, but instead I was greeted by the sight of her sitting upright beside me! "Mother!" I exclaimed. "You're still here!"

"I've always been here, sweetheart," she purred.

"What do you mean by that?" I was angry again. But before I could confront her further, Sarahil knocked on the palanquin base, asking if she could draw the curtains to prepare me for nighttime camp.

"Sarahil, look who's here!" I said excitedly. She and Mother had been best friends.

Sarahil blinked and looked around my room, then she chuckled and shook her head. "It's been a long day, Queen Makeda," she said, reaching her hand up to mine and helping me to the ground. I looked over at Mother, who grinned, winked, and followed us.

"Sarahil, did you see that Mother's here?"

Sarahil politely pretended not to hear me. She was being kind to avoid embarrassing me. Was it possible that Sarahil couldn't *see* Mother?

We dined on *misser wot,* a delicious spicy lentil stew, around the campfire. Many of our meals during the journey incorporated dried beans, the easiest protein source to carry over the hot desert roads.

Mother sat right next to me for the entire meal. She wouldn't take a plate of food, but she did use her fingers to nibble on some of mine—yet she couldn't have been eating the actual food, because no matter how much she took from my plate, the same amount remained. It almost looked as if she were eating the *shadow* of the lentils and sauce!

"I'm consuming the essence of the food," she explained. "At my vibrational level, I don't need physical food, but I do enjoy its flavor and energy, so that's what I'm absorbing. Purely for entertainment, mind you."

Well, I also found food quite "entertaining," but I couldn't imagine just inhaling it. I needed to chew and feel its substance in my belly in order to feel satisfied. I watched Mother's blissful expression as she put the *misser wot* into her mouth. Okay, she *was* chewing and swallowing, but it just wasn't the same as eating solid food.

I stared into the campfire, hypnotized by the flames' dancing blue tips. Mother leaned over and said, "If they see you talking to me, they'll wonder whether the journey and heat is too much for you, since no one but you can see me." Just then, a young boy about three years old walked up to Mother and stared with wide eyes. "Well, the *adults* can't see me," she added with a wink.

I stifled a giggle so Sarahil wouldn't worry about my mental health. Fortunately, she and Tamrin were engaged in lively discussions about the next day's travel schedule. From the looks of it, Tamrin was definitely winning the argument, but was doing so in his true diplomatic and inoffensive style.

"Honey, I realize you're angry that I left you and your father," Mother began. I bit my lip and swallowed hard. "Please understand that I've never *truly* left you. I've always been right by your side, helping, guiding, and even rescuing you. Remember that time you took the chariot out on your own? Who do you think cushioned your fall when it tilted to one side after the camel was spooked by that bird?"

I *did* remember that day! As the chariot had violently tipped to the left, I'd felt as if an invisible pair of strong arms carried me away and gently set me by the road. I'd always wondered what had happened. But that still didn't explain why Mother was suddenly appearing to me now.

"Then how come I haven't seen you until recently?" I demanded to know. People around the campfire looked at me with quizzical expressions, wondering whom I was talking to.

"Just *think* your questions, Makeda. I can hear your thoughts. Anyway, to answer your question, you weren't ready to use your visual sense of connecting with me," she replied cryptically. Compassion flashed across Mother's face, and she continued: "Even though you didn't see me, you always *felt* my presence, didn't you?"

I thought about the night Father had died. Even though he'd been ill a long time and we all knew he'd die eventually, I was unprepared for how sad and alone I felt when he actually passed. I'd sobbed for Mother that night. I recalled how a warm blanket of energy— a presence—followed. I'd thought I was imagining that experience and countless others that I only vaguely recalled at the moment.

"So that really was you?" I held my breath until she nodded, and then I exhaled with relief to know that she hadn't abandoned me as I'd feared. I wanted to hug her right then and there, but she motioned toward the others around the campfire: It was all about appearances when you were a queen. We moved a short distance away from the others—I preferred to be able to speak aloud to Mother and interact with her unobserved.

"This was one of the reasons why I *had* to disappear," Mother explained. "The strain of pretending to be a noblewoman was eroding my physical health and happiness. Everyone expected the queen to act in a certain way—to be perfect, really. But the biggest stressor was the jealousy, competition, and backstabbing from people who were trying to manipulate me and use my royal title to further their own selfish interests. Remember how sick I was? Those were symptoms of all the anger and sadness I held inside of my body. You, Tamrin, Sarahil, and your father were the only people of pure intention I met in my mortal life."

"In your 'mortal' life?" I wanted to fully understand what Mother was saying.

"Yes, when I took on human form after helping your father slay the dragon," she confirmed. "We fell in love, and I couldn't return to my original Jinn form. I fell under the spell of living up to his—and all of the other humans'—expectations of what I should look and act like. I truly lost myself during that time period. But it didn't matter, because you were there to keep me sane, happy, and grounded."

"Then why did you leave me, Mother?" I had to know whether she'd gone because of something I'd done wrong, because she didn't love me anymore, or for some even more horrible reason. Besides, since Mother was reading my thoughts, there was no way I could hide my fears from her.

"Honey, I didn't leave. I just went upward to a higher dimension that most people can't see. You can see me now because this journey has increased your connection to nature, fresh air, and sunshine. The great outdoors has elevated your spiritual vibrations, which has allowed you to connect to me easily and naturally. Let me help you get in conscious touch with this higher vibration."

Mother's image grew fainter until she disappeared. I could still hear her voice, though. "Close your eyes, sweet Makeda. Breathe deeply and focus on the feelings around your head and shoulders," she coached.

I did as she directed but didn't notice anything. I started to panic that maybe I hadn't inherited my mother's spiritual gifts. *What if I couldn't feel or see any-thing?*

"*Everyone* is spiritually gifted, honey!" I forgot that Mother could hear my thoughts. She gently coaxed me to close my eyes again and inhale deeply. As I exhaled, Mother advised, "Don't try so hard, and keep your thoughts really positive. Hold the assumption that you'll be able to feel my presence and your optimism will always be rewarded."

I followed her instructions and noticed a sensation of thick warmth, like a comfortable blanket, around my shoulders. I relaxed into the feeling, leaning forward with my eyes closed. Then the campfire crackled loudly and I snapped back into conscious awareness. Maybe I was just imagining the sensations?

"You weren't imagining them, sweetheart. I'm right here, hugging your shoulders. Now tune in again."

My mind reeled. But Mother had passed away! I must be going mad, hallucinating from the desert heat!

Mother's image solidified again, and I felt her arm steady me as I leaned toward her. "That's enough for tonight, honey," she said comfortingly. I never wanted the moment to end.

👑 👑 👑

CHAPTER 8

When I awoke, Mother was gone, but the wrinkled sheets and indented pillow next to mine told me that her visit wasn't just a dream. I felt the familiar pang in my heart stemming from her absence, and for a moment guilt shrouded me as I wrestled with anger toward her cavalier style of coming and going in and out of my life. *I should feel grateful that she visited me!* I told myself. Still, my stomach tightened as I wondered when I might see her again.

I put Mother out of my mind by keeping my palanquin's curtains open and enjoying the desert landscape. The rolling sand dunes were decorated with the smoothest windblown lines, as if a giant cat had run sharp claws across each mound. Occasionally, little flowers and desert animals made appearances, but mostly the only changes in scenery involved the sun's trajectory.

The sunsets were glorious and awe-inspiring bursts of color, each one giving us hope that the next day's travels would be easier. Our journey had been long and arduous. I had no idea how long we'd been away from home, nor how much farther our destination was. A part of me didn't *want* to know.

I looked forward to our meals, our daily sun worship in the afternoon, and sleeping. The in-between moments, though, were a test of endurance. My body felt sore from too many days of sitting on my bed cushion. Yet I didn't dare complain, because everyone else's situation was worse. At least I could lie down during the day, out of the heat. The others had to sit on camel saddles—or worse, walk.

I couldn't believe that Tamrin had traveled this route so frequently. Of course, he'd never brought a caravan of this size, a fact that we were reminded of as our food and water supply dwindled. Apparently, Tamrin hadn't planned for enough meals on our long trek. We implored Almaqah and Athtar to provide us with sufficient food and water to stay healthy.

One morning I was awakened by a commotion. I pulled back the flaps of my tent to see Tamrin and some other men kneeling over a camel who was lying on the ground. The animal grunted, and out came a perfect little baby camel! I blinked at this marvel, having never witnessed a birth before. One of the men cleaned up the baby, and the mother camel got to her feet immediately to tend to her little one herself.

I worried how the baby camel would make it through the desert, but I should have known that Tamrin would have a plan. He hoisted the baby atop the back of the camel who walked in front of the mother camel. That way, she had a steady view of her son while they were walking!

How I envied that mother camel! The animals were so free of restrictions. I, on the other hand, had to live by a fistful of rules, which included staying virginal my entire life because of my marriage to a sun god whose hand I would never feel. I exhaled deeply, wishing my mother were there so that I could learn more about my own childhood and why I had to be the queen.

That night, I had difficulty falling asleep. Maybe I was napping too much during the day, or perhaps the spicy food made my metabolism work overtime. I felt hot, so I tossed off my blanket. I tried fluffing the pillow to get comfortable, but that didn't work either. *It's useless to try sleeping,* I decided. I'm wide-awake and might as well take a walk in the fresh night air.

The guard outside my tent had fallen asleep, so I easily walked past him. Once again I silently thanked Abby, my beautiful cat whom I missed so much, for her lessons on how to move quietly.

When I was away from the campground, I relaxed and slowed my pace to that of a walking meditation to try to calm myself so that I could sleep. The moon- and starlight cast dazzling bluish white shadows across the sand dunes and rocks. The shadows seemed to move as I walked, and for a moment I thought I saw my mother with a group of petite people against one of the rocks. I blinked, and realized that I must have imagined it.

I sat against the rocks and stared at the sky. More than anything I wanted to feel satisfied and happy, yet my gnawing emptiness told me that something was missing from my life. But what could it be? I closed my eyes and prayed to Hawbas, the goddess of Venus: "Hawbas, please help me to feel fulfilled!"

I opened my eyes just in time to see a shooting star arc overhead. As its tail moved toward the campground, I thought that I should do the same. Hawbas's sign made me feel comfortable—I didn't need my mother, a husband, or a baby to feel complete! I was a strong, competent woman who was making a difference to my commonwealth. I could attain fulfillment on my own, thank you very much.

When I returned to my tent, the temperature seemed just right and my pillows felt comfortable. I fell asleep immediately and was so relaxed that I felt some minor annoyance when *he* showed up! I really just wanted to sleep, not get all excited and passionate. Fortunately, he was in the same mood, so we just snuggled together—that is, until Mother showed up, stomped, and yelled *"No!"* just as she had the last time he and I had embraced.

I woke up to find Mother standing over me, her arms folded defiantly across her chest. "Makeda, you cannot allow this romance to continue!"

"But Mother, it's just a dream. It's not real!"

"*Everything* is real, Makeda. Or have you forgotten this key element of your Jinn nature?"

"Mother, I don't know *anything* about my Jinn nature!"

Mother breathed deeply and looked down. She seemed to search for the right spot on which to sit. I patted my hand next to my pillow as a peace-offering invitation.

Mother sat and looked me straight in the eyes. "It will change your life, Makeda."

"What will, Mother?"

"The teachings of the Jinn folk," she said solemnly. Her tone of voice made me wonder if I was better off remaining ignorant about the Jinn ways. But then I felt my feet scrape against my blanket, and I realized that Sarahil hadn't been able to shave or oil them properly since we'd left home several months earlier.

"Mother, why do our feet have to look so ugly? Aren't the Jinn able to shift into any shape they want?"

Mother stroked my feet lovingly and put her own next to mine: They were nearly identical. "Why, honey, these feet are beautiful! They're gorgeous! They're perfect for walking across any terrain, climbing any tree or bush, or carrying heavy objects. In our land, our feet are a symbol of beauty."

"Not in the humans' land, Mother," I sighed, covering my feet with my blanket.

"Well, I can teach you how to influence human perceptions so that no one notices your feet," Mother offered.

I accepted gratefully, and Mother cupped her hands in the direction of my feet, which grew warm and then hot. I danced in place to disperse the heat, but Mother insisted that I stand still. Soon, the energy Mother was sending to my feet radiated like the wispy rays that create mirages across desert sands. Mother kept breathing intently, and the radiant heat grew into light that completely masked my feet. I could no longer see them; all I could see were two balls of light!

I begged Mother to show me the secret, and she held my hands together so that my thumbs were parallel, the tips of my index fingers touched, and my palms were open. Mother pointed my cupped hands downward toward my feet and told me to breathe in and out deeply while imagining a fire. "Breathe in the flames!" she coached. "Then see them building inside of you and coming out of your hands."

My hands felt very hot, so I shook them to cool them down. Mother grabbed them and said, "Focus!" in a way that let me know that I needed to take this lesson seriously.

I resumed my deep breathing while visualizing one of Tamrin's blazing campfires. Then it occurred to me that the sun was much hotter than a mere campfire, so I silently called upon Almaqah for some real heat. *"Ouch!"* I yelped. My invocation had worked *too* well!

"Focus, Makeda," said Mother. "Don't try to make anything happen. Just focus on the fire, as if you were really there with it. Feel the heat of it; smell its smoke; and especially see its brightness, colors, and movement."

I saw the campfire's yellow and blue fingers dance inside my body and out through my hands. I put my entire concentration on the fire, as Mother had advised.

"Now, Makeda, hold the thought of transferring the light of the fire to render your feet invisible. You don't need to do anything else. Just instruct the fire within you, telling it what you desire."

It was that simple? I'd always thought that Jinn magic was complicated and formula driven. As I pondered this question, I lost sight of the flames and my hands cooled.

"Focus!" Mother snapped.

I breathed and began again, conjuring the image, feelings, and smells of the campfire. I breathed in this impression, to consume the fire's essence. Then I told it that I wanted its light to block the sight of my feet. My hands grew warm, then intensely hot. I held them steady and focused on the vision and intention. Slowly, I opened my eyes and shrieked when I saw the two balls of light hovering over my feet. "I did it, Mother!"

"Why of course you did, sweetheart. I never doubted your abilities at all."

Mother continued to teach me to work with the energy of light and fire every evening after the others had gone to bed. She didn't need to sneak around about our meetings, since I was the only adult who could see or hear her, but we kept our reunions clandestine because my talking to Mother would appear as if I were speaking to a hallucination.

My anger at Mother's "death" was diminishing, and I felt that I was regaining a lost part of my soul as she and I once again became close friends. She was a wonderful teacher, and I even learned how to increase the ball of light in order to create total invisibility (which was a great skill that allowed me to avoid Tamrin's and Sarahil's watchful eyes).

I asked Mother why we worked with fire so much, and she surprised me by explaining that the Jinn were created from fire.

"All beings originated from one of the four basic elements of earth, air, water, or fire merged with the fifth element of Spirit," she said. "Humans are composed of the earth element, which means that they're dependent upon material needs, and their energy is denser and heavier. Merbeings, who live in the oceans and rivers, are composed of water energy. And the angels are from the energy of air."

Tamrin had briefly mentioned angels when he'd discussed King Solomon, but I still didn't understand what they were, so I asked Mother to explain. She mumbled something about how I'd learn about angels soon enough, and then very pointedly changed the subject. I knew better than to pry for information when Mother didn't want to talk—but I did wonder about these angels of the air, so I decided to see if Tamrin knew anything more. After all, he was a man of the world who'd learned much during his travels.

"Angels, eh?" Tamrin squinted at me, the campfire casting eerie shadows across his face. He was silent for so long that I regretted asking him about a topic so obviously secret that even my own mother wouldn't discuss it.

"Well, the only thing I've heard about angels is that King Solomon works very closely with them. What was the name of that angel he works especially closely with? . . . Oh yes—Michael."

Michael. The name brought shudders to my body, as if my cells knew something from a deep-seated memory. "What does this Michael angel do for Solomon?" I asked, not quite sure if that was really my question, but wanting to encourage Tamrin to keep talking.

"From what I understand, it's what *Solomon* does for Michael," Tamrin said slowly. "Now my knowledge of angels is restricted to hearsay, and my understanding of the Hebrew language—which is what you'll hear most people speak in Jerusalem—is limited."

Hebrew! I barely knew anything about the language! I worried whether this whole journey to Jerusalem had been a mistake.

In answer to my unspoken question, Tamrin reassured me that King Solomon was proficient in our Sabaean tongue. We'd have no trouble communicating. Then he added, "Remember that the God of Israel gave King Solomon complete power to rule and communicate with all people, animals, birds, angels, and demons. I've even heard that the angel Michael gave King Solomon a special ring that he uses to control seventy-two demons who are building his temple! He points his ring in their direction, and the demons fall completely under the king's control."

"Demons! That's a derogatory term for the Djinn!" I interjected without trying to control the hurt in my voice. This King Solomon sounded like a very insensitive person. Maybe I wouldn't be able to communicate with him after all, no matter how many languages he spoke.

I was never sure how much Tamrin knew about my mother and my Jinn heritage. It seemed like a taboo topic and was rarely mentioned, even when Sarahil was treating my feet. This always made me feel ashamed of my culture, as if there was something wrong with it. And when someone used the "demon" slur, I positively cowered. The Jinn were so misunderstood!

Tamrin put his arm around me to reassure and calm me. He knew better than anyone that when my temper was invoked, I acted and spoke impulsively, like a little child. Mother had explained the importance of watching myself when I was angry, lest I throw "fireballs" at people. I was still working with her on that lesson.

Finally Tamrin spoke, so gently that it was almost a whisper. His voice was melodious, with accents of the various languages and cultures he'd experienced. I truly admired and loved him with all of my heart.

"Now you know that when people use that term"—he didn't want to say *demons* and risk upsetting me again—"they're referring to the other type of Djinn," Tamrin reminded me. "Almost everyone knows that the Jinn are the wisest, purest, and most trustworthy of all the Djinn. Those who don't know this are just plain ignorant and not worth listening to anyway."

Tamrin was right. Jinn were just one type of being lumped into the Djinn category. The other types were troublemakers, giving us a bad name. That is, unless someone knew that the Shaytan Djinn were distinct from us lovable Jinn.

Was it time for us to change our names and break away from the whole Djinn category? I sighed with exhaustion at the thought of this momentous public-relations campaign. Better to just settle it in my own mind. Mother said you couldn't control what other people thought, so why waste your time and energy?

That evening, Mother slept next to me, without giving me instructions or lessons beforehand. She must have sensed how tired I was after journeying for nearly three full-moon cycles. I had desert-sand dust in every crevice of my palanquin, and the gritty texture was always in my mouth. I was cranky and wanted to return home to my own bed, my cat, and sand-free meals!

Apparently, Mother felt that the easiest way to calm me was to enter into my dreams. Soon after I fell asleep, she and I sat in my beloved courtyard on the palace grounds back in Saba. A cool breeze wafted, bringing floral fragrances, as she explained to me that I had a very important life purpose to fulfill in Jerusalem. It was essential for me to meet King Solomon, she emphasized, and not to get sidetracked by emotions (including any attractions to other men).

She explained my life purpose in great detail, but I could only remember fragments of what she said upon awakening. And Mother feigned ignorance when I pressed her to repeat the details while I was awake. Finally she said, "Our dreams contain fourth-dimensional information, which cannot be processed by our conscious three-dimensional minds!" and I knew it was time to let the entire topic go.

All I knew was that my Mother, and some unknowable force, was drawing me to Jerusalem . . . and to King Solomon, his angels, and his Djinn.

CHAPTER 9

It had been another restless night. Although I was excited about meeting King Solomon and intrigued to learn about his angels, the discomfort of travel was taking its toll on my body. I just couldn't seem to get comfortable, no matter how many pillows I stuffed beneath my bottom! The man of my dreams hadn't visited since Mother's last interruption, so I'd even lost that escape.

I didn't know how many more days I could take of sunlight blaring across endless sand dunes! I wasn't the only travel-weary person in our caravan either. The others looked bedraggled, and there still wasn't enough food and water for the remaining journey. What would we do?

One night, our beloved god Athtar mercifully sent us a rain shower. Our tents blew over and we were all soaked, but no one really minded. Everyone—including the camels and donkeys—blissfully bathed in the rain while Tamrin's crew filled buckets with the sweet liquid. We were finally reassured that all of the animals and people in our caravan would have enough to drink.

Mother continued giving me lessons about Jinn magic. I learned how to direct the fire's light to disinfect wounds, water, food, and anything else that needed sterilization. I stopped throwing fireballs when I was angry, and instead used the anger's energy to direct the situation toward my desired outcome.

For instance, one night I was awakened by Tamrin's men laughing and singing loudly. I stewed in my resentment, not wanting to disrupt their party, but instead feeling victimized by their noise. This resentment, Mother taught me, was like throwing spears of hot fire in their direction. I wouldn't have known this, except that the men all complained of backaches the next morning. That's when Mother said that my fire spears had become a pain in their backs!

She made me undo my fire spears by visualizing water vapors as a big, beautiful blue light. Mother had me inhale the blue radiance and then direct it out of my palms and fingers onto their backs, to cool away their fiery pain just like water extinguishing flames.

Many of my Jinn lessons were like that, where Mother taught me to take responsibility for my feelings. "Emotions are pure power, Makeda," she said repeatedly. "Channel that pure power in your desired direction and you'll never feel like a victim again!"

I'd look for loopholes in this philosophy, but each time, Mother showed me how I could direct my visualization of the fire and couple it with my strong emotions to create desirable effects. Once, when Tamrin had trouble lighting the campfire, I peered out of my tent and sent fire energy until it ignited. Tamrin never realized, nor would I ever admit, that I'd lit the fire.

Whenever I'd feel sorry for myself, Mother would remind me to take charge of the situation. With her help, I was able to redirect resentment and frustration in positive ways. Yet, there were a couple of situations that I didn't vocalize to her, because I realized that Jinn magic couldn't alter them.

"Such as?" Mother asked.

Darn! I kept forgetting that she could hear my thoughts! Okay, why not give it a try and explain my feelings about this way-too-long journey to her?

Mother listened sympathetically as I expressed my anguish over the monotonous days of travel through the endless desert. I had no sense that we were getting any closer to Jerusalem, only that my eyes, mouth, and hair were forever filled with sand!

"Honey, I'm waiting for you to form your complaints into a Statement of Empowerment!"

That phrase! Mother continually said that every worry, complaint, or problem could be reworded into what she called a *Statement of Empowerment*. "Clearly decide what your ultimate dream outcome would be," she'd say. "Then reword that dream into a definitive statement that this is what you expect the Universe to deliver to you right now."

Instead of empathizing with me about my long journey to Jerusalem, Mother urged me, "Take charge and do something about the situation, Makeda! As long as you complain, you etch your victimhood as an absolute factor that can't be changed. But with the Statement of Empowerment, you regain the ability to experience a different, more favorable outcome."

"You mean I'd learn to enjoy the travel?" I asked.

"Well, that would be one solution. What outcome would be even more desirable, though?" Mother's style of teaching was to answer with a question.

I couldn't even voice it, because it seemed too far-fetched even for Jinn magic. Mother stared at me until I finally said it: "I want the journey to be over so that we're already in Jerusalem!" There! The words were uttered!

"Congratulations, Makeda. You've just made your Statement of Empowerment!"

Mother had known this was possible all along, but she'd waited until I hit rock bottom as far as my patience with the never-ending desert journey was concerned. I begged Mother to show me how to magically transport our caravan to Jerusalem. Now that my appetite was whetted, I couldn't bear another night in my tent!

"Please, Mother!" I insisted.

Mother hissed that I was giving my power away to her. She said that anything she could do, I could do, too. Well, this was the last thing I wanted to hear, so I rolled over on the bed and turned my back toward her, while tears streamed down my face. Maybe this whole journey had been one giant mistake!

I felt Mother's hand on my shoulder, but I jerked away from it. If she really loved me, she'd rescue me from this terrible ordeal! I fell asleep and dreamed that Mother and Tamrin were cooking *kik alitcha* chickpea stew over the campfire. They both pointed to the smoke drifting in the nighttime breeze. I followed the smoke's journey until it floated into the dark sky.

The smoke! I sat up and saw Mother grinning like a wizard. "*Now* do you understand, Makeda?" she stroked my hair.

"I think so, Mother." I cautiously summarized my understanding of working with the smoke of the fire to alter our vibrations so we could travel faster, more smoothly, and farther.

"Yes, that's a part of it," Mother confirmed. "The same element of fire, which you've had so much success with, will also grant your wish for instant travel. Smoke can go along the path of subtle energies. And so can the sun's rays, which travel great distances at light speed."

The sun's rays! Almaqah! Why hadn't I thought of this earlier?

"You were too busy complaining and feeling sorry for yourself," Mother answered my thoughts. I wondered if I'd ever be able to read minds as she did.

"Of course! You can do it right now!" she replied. She faced me and held my hands. "Now start with a Statement of Empowerment that you can already read minds."

I mumbled something to myself about mind reading.

"Make it clear and positive!" Mother snapped. Then her voice softened: "Sorry, honey, I just want you to get this lesson, which you're already so close to understanding."

I wondered whether I could effectively learn with a tired, foggy mind. But at Mother's insistence, I kept rewording and reciting my Statement of Empowerment until I could really feel its power coming through my mind and body.

"I easily tap into the messages and helpful information that other people are thinking. I use this skill in the name of love, healing, and blessings for all!" I said with conviction.

Mother then told me to watch her and match her breathing rate. She closed her eyes, and her chest went up and down with each inhalation and exhalation. I mimicked her deep breathing and watched my own chest rise and fall. Soon, the sounds of our breath were in sync.

"Keep the same rate of breathing while you listen to what's next, Makeda," she counseled me. "Once the rate is matched, you next ask a mental question that you would like the answer to. For example, you can ask, *What are you thinking?* or *How can I help?*"

Mother closed her eyes again, and I ensured that our breathing was in unison before shutting mine and mentally asking, *Do you love me?* I immediately heard, *Of course! Now ask something else.*

I opened my eyes and saw Mother staring at me with a big impish smile. We both fell over laughing before we continued doing mind reading, which I easily mastered once I overcame my intimidation. And with practice, I gained more confidence that I might actually read humans' minds!

Over the next few days, Mother worked with me to further my abilities as far as channeling sunlight with my hands and making the Statements of Empowerment. I cupped my hands around the balls of light with thumbs on top and pointed them toward small targets such as leaves and rocks. I then made Statements of Empowerment that the objects would travel along the sun's rays to the intended location.

The first time I tried this, the leaf caught on fire! Mother guided me to cup my hands only partially toward my object, with the majority of the sun's rays pointed in the direction I intended the object to travel. This time it worked! I was able to transport a leaf quite a distance—somehow it appeared instantly across the campsite. (I knew that it was the same leaf because of its distinctive markings.) It didn't float through the air; rather, it dissolved in front of me and reappeared where Mother stood.

Through trial and error, I had the same success transporting rocks. I had to overcome my belief that rocks were heavy and would need more energy to relocate. Once Mother explained that all objects weigh the same from an energetic standpoint, I treated them as if they were identical to the leaves I'd transported earlier.

One day Mother said that I was ready to transport a camel. I balked at this, thinking that I needed extra instruction to move a living being. Mother talked me through this belief. "All physical objects are composed of the same particles and energies," she emphasized. "Besides, rocks and leaves are just as alive as a camel or a person."

Once I overcame my mental blocks, the camel's transportation proved just as simple as that of the leaves and rocks. Mother remarked, "You can apply the same magical principles to transport entire buildings filled with people."

After I'd practiced moving a tent, several camels, and a chariot, Mother had me practice transporting *her*. I again had to remove limiting beliefs, including nervousness at harming or disappointing her. With Mother's reassurance that only good things would occur, I successfully transported her from the campsite to the foothills.

When she returned to my side, Mother looked at me with big soulful brown eyes, a signal that she had something important to say. "Honey, you said that there were two things on your mind, one of them being the long journey. We'll take care of that issue tomorrow at noon. What's the second concern you'd like to address?"

I explained my desire to have a flesh-and-blood husband and children of my own. "But I'm married to the sun god, and I'm supposed to stay a virgin during my royal reign!" I complained.

"That doesn't sound like a Statement of Empowerment to me," Mother scolded.

I couldn't believe that her Statements of Empowerment could work on *everything*. Surely this was the exception. But Mother coaxed me through taking the seeming problem, turning it around, and making it into a positive declaration: "I am happily married to a wonderful mortal man; and we have one or more beautiful, healthy children."

Then she announced, "Your life purpose will be revealed, and that in itself will resolve this entire situation. Have no worries, Makeda. You *will* have a child and a husband, and you will still be Queen of Sheba."

I knew better than to press Mother for more details when she spoke so intently. Still, I was bouncing up and down with excitement inside and secretly hoping for more information about this topic. I didn't know how it would all occur, but I trusted Mother's wisdom and insight. For now, I tried to sleep. Tomorrow we would be in Jerusalem!

CHAPTER 10

When I awoke the next morning, it was obvious that Tamrin, Sarahil, and our caravan crew regarded it as just an ordinary day. They had no idea of the magic that was in store for them.

I set about packing my belongings with extra enthusiasm and ate heartily at breakfast. Sarahil remarked that I was in a better mood than she'd seen for a while, and I had to agree. I desperately wanted to reveal the reason for my happiness, but then I remembered that I'd promised Mother not to discuss Jinn magic with humans.

Mother was already in my palanquin when I climbed inside for the start of our day's journey. Our plan was to perform the teleportation when our caravan stopped for our afternoon sun worship, so I figured Mother was there to relax for the next few hours with me. Instead, though, she seemed intent on working.

She announced, "We need to work on your riddles before you get to Jerusalem."

"Excuse me?" I coughed. Then I recalled the female voice that had cryptically said "riddles" several months earlier when I'd felt insecure about conversing with King Solomon. "Mother, what are you up to now?" I demanded to know.

She explained that the king was a connoisseur of mental gymnastics. He enjoyed *koans* (Asian-inspired stories that require intuitive rather than rational thought to understand); puzzles; and most of all, riddles. Mother said that the king would see me as a peer and intellectual equal if I prepared riddles for him. "They will be a more appreciated gift than all the gold, lumber, gems, and spices you're hauling across the desert for him," she added.

Since riddles weren't my strong suit, I was glad that Mother offered to coach me. "I'll be right by your side the entire visit," she promised, "whispering in your ear when you need my guidance."

Soon it was noon, and the caravan stopped for our daily time of worship. Our people were often referred to as "sun worshipers," but then humans generalize and oversimplify religious practices that they don't understand, don't they?

In truth, our worship consisted of giving thanks and praise to all of the life-giving aspects of nature, which included the sun, moon, stars, water, cattle, air, and so on. When we offered gratitude for these things, more blessings from nature always came our way. Our religious practices were one reason why Saba was among the most prosperous and peaceful of all the kingdoms in Arabia, Africa, and Asia!

The priests unrolled our portable temple, which consisted of a cloth large enough for all of the people in our caravan to kneel down, statues of our pantheon of deities, and incense holders, where we offered frankincense and myrrh to the heavens. The priests read invocations, we all chanted in succession to each deity, and afterward everyone ate—for once, we stopped long enough to have lunch.

As the others enjoyed their meals, Mother and I stood by the midday campfire. She insisted that I perform the transportation ceremony on my own, so I first called upon Almaqah to calm my nervousness and help me focus.

I then used the methods Mother had taught me that had successfully transported leaves, rocks, and even a camel during my practice sessions. I cupped my hands and brought my thumbs together and drew the smoke of the fire into them. I then called upon the sun's rays and made my Statement of Empowerment that the entire caravan—including all the people, animals, and items we carried—be transported along the smoke and the sun's rays to King Solomon's palace gate. I breathed deeply and held this vision with my eyes shut until Mother gently asked me to open them.

Everyone was in their previous positions, eating and resting . . . but the scenery had changed! We were now just outside a cascading bank of palatial walls, gates, and dozens of huge alabaster pillars, each with a girth wider than Tamrin's belly!

A parade of men on camels and donkeys rode toward us, obviously alarmed by our sudden presence. Tamrin stood up, looked around with a puzzled expression, grabbed our flag of Sheba, and walked up to meet the men.

By now, the rest of the caravan had noticed our change of venue. Most of the men looked frozen with fear, but some scrambled to don shields and swords. A few were kneeling in prayerful positions, appealing to Almaqah's mercy.

Tamrin signaled for me to join him, and I wondered if one of those present was King Solomon. Since my Hebrew was limited, Tamrin translated.

"Dear Queen of Sheba," the lead man said, bowing deeply, "we weren't expecting your arrival for several months! But of course, you're very welcome here in our kingdom. Our ladies will escort you and your handmaiden to your chambers so that you may rest and be refreshed prior to meeting King Solomon."

I curtsied in return and gladly left the caravan with Sarahil. Mother was by my side, although no one could see her but me, the camels, and a handful of young children. Four beautiful young women dressed in colorful gauzy gowns led us through a gate in the back of the palace so that we could enter the citadel discreetly in our dirty travel-weary clothing. This would allow Sarahil and me to polish our appearance prior to our official entrance to the kingdom.

I waved good-bye to Sarahil as we were led to separate chambers. A large sudsy tub that smelled like heaven awaited me. The chamber attendants, who didn't speak my language (nor I theirs) held up a robe and pointed to an area where I could take off my clothing in privacy. I noticed one of the women staring at my feet as I returned to the bathing area. She smiled kindly and motioned that she could file my toenails for me. I nodded gratefully.

"Ahh!" The tub's water was just the right degree of warmth; and the fragrance of jasmine, rose, and sandalwood helped me relax. A thin young woman with a pretty complexion began washing my hair with a citrus-smelling compound. My tresses definitely needed attention, after who-knew-how-many months of desert travel. The hot air, sandstorms, lack of proper bathing, and stress had turned my normally beautiful mane into a tangled and dirty mess.

While my scalp was being massaged, the other woman lifted my left foot. I had to quickly turn on my side to avoid having my head slide under the water.

Both women giggled, and I watched gratefully as the second woman filed my toenails, applied oil, and shaved my feet. I really needed this spa treatment!

After the bath, I was led to a small rock-wall room, which was warm but not so hot that sweat would undo my bath and shampoo. An older woman whose hair was pulled back into a tight bun carried a basket filled with alabaster and calcite bottles and jars. She sat on a chair beside me and indicated that she was going to give me a facial. I closed my eyes and surrendered to her gentle motions and the delicious aromas of her lotions and oils. . . .

When I awoke, I was no longer on the facialist's table but on a real bed, thick with padding—which I appreciated after so many months of thin travel mattresses during our journey. I suddenly missed my cat, Abby, very much and craned my head to see if Sarahil was anywhere around. She wasn't . . . but Mother was. "Sleep well, kitten?" she asked while stroking my newly silky hair.

I rubbed my eyes and noticed the gorgeous chamber around me. It was three times the size of my bedroom back home, and the shiny wooden walls were ornately decorated with golden carved flowers. The bed, which was big enough for five people, had a golden-peach silk headboard and matching bedcover. The colors were definitely more subdued than in Saba, where my room sported pillows of rainbow hues.

"How long did I sleep, Mother?"

"A full day," she answered.

"You're awake!" Sarahil's cheery voice greeted me as she entered with a colorful plate of fruit and breads. She looked rested and freshly scrubbed. I nibbled while Sarahil described her spa treatment, a luxury she usually gave me, but rarely received herself.

Mother rubbed Sarahil's back, who leaned into the pleasurable sensation. Mother said, "She can't see me, but she *can* feel my energy." Apparently Sarahil couldn't hear Mother either.

The older woman who'd performed my facial opened a door to another room and motioned for us to follow her. The room was actually a walk-in closet filled with every imaginable color of gown, scarf, and headpiece. The woman held an iris-violet gown in front of me, nodded with approval, and handed it to her young assistant. Sarahil was outfitted in a blue-gray dress befitting her age and status, as well as flattering her hair and complexion.

After we were thoroughly groomed—our makeup applied and hair and clothing arranged—we were ushered into a lobby, where Tamrin was sitting. He also looked—and smelled—like a new man! We hugged each other gingerly so as not to muss our attire. Mother also embraced Tamrin, who looked in her direction for reasons I'm sure he couldn't understand.

Two guards smiled at us tensely, as if they were uncomfortable in their uniforms. "They're taking us to see the king," Tamrin translated their words in a whisper, as if it were a secret. A whooshing sound passed through my ears and I felt light-headed. I wasn't ready to meet King Solomon. Not yet.

Mother held me so that I wouldn't faint. The two uniformed men kept marching, unaware that we'd slowed our pace. Soon the men were around the bend of a long corridor, and I didn't know if we'd find our way through the palace's maze of hallways and doors. Tamrin found a bench where I could sit, and he wiped beads of perspiration from my forehead. "Just take your time, Queen Balkis. There's no hurry at all," he reassured me—then I blacked out.

I woke up on the bench, with my head in Sarahil's lap. The guards stood over me, talking anxiously. They motioned to a nearby servant woman, who asked (with Tamrin translating) if she could escort me back to my chamber to rest. I stood, and again felt faint. Sitting, I put my hand to my heart and felt the stone pendant that my father had given to me. A surge of energy pushed me back to my feet, and my head felt tingly, but this time in a positive, life-affirming way.

"I'm ready to meet the king," I announced, forcing my voice to sound more confident than I really felt. Tamrin and Sarahil looked at me questioningly, and I nodded to reassure them that I was fine.

As we followed the uniformed men, I clutched the dragon bloodstone pendant in my right hand. My chest rose and fell and my heart pounded. Perspiration made my silk dress stick to my skin. I hoped that I looked suitable for King Solomon.

Guards announced our arrival, and our pace quickened as they ceremoniously opened two enormous carved doors. I gingerly followed the others through the entrance, still unsure if I really wanted to meet the king. But I'd come this far and was anxious to confront him about his ungracious invitation—that is, if I could work up the courage.

I saw a golden glow in the distance ahead of us, and I realized that the king sat on an elaborate gilded throne elevated on a stage platform. In front of it was a beautiful reflecting pond. Hundreds of orange and white koi fish swam like an energetic audience for him.

I was escorted to the front of our group. Tamrin and Sarahil signaled that it was safe for me to proceed without them. But how to approach the king with this enormous pool separating me and his throne? The water looked shallow enough, but couldn't I just walk *around* the pond to meet him?

The guards extended their hands and pointed, indicating that I was indeed to walk through the pond to reach the king. I wasn't happy about this one bit! After all that I'd gone through to travel to see him, the least he could do would be to get off of his darned throne and come meet me!

But the guards kept insisting, and Tamrin and Sarahil nodded their tense approval. I sighed and surrendered to the situation.

I removed my shoes and lifted the hem of my skirt to keep them from getting wet, and then I put one foot in the pond. But instead of wetness, I only felt a cool hardness beneath it. Why, the pond was covered by an enormous sheet of clear crystal!

Horrified, I realized that when I'd removed my shoes and lifted my hem, I'd displayed my Jinn feet, which weren't something that I'd planned to reveal to King Solomon and his court. So I quickly cupped my palms and focused on drawing firelight through them until a hot spotlight of brightness covered my feet. As I walked the rest of the distance, the crystal floor amplified the light, creating so much heat that I had to step high to cool my feet. The illumination was so intense that it covered my legs from the knees downward.

The king stood and descended from his elaborate ivory-and-gold throne. Its back was carved to resemble an enormous bull, and it was guarded by a tremendous gilded lion statue. More fierce golden lion statues graced each side of the six steps leading from the stage to the palace floor.

King Solomon was tall, perhaps the tallest man I'd ever seen . . . or maybe his incredible charisma made him seem larger-than-life. He wore heavy white silk pants, and a purple and gold brocade shirt, which was perfectly tailored to his muscular chest and slim waist. His skin was lighter than mine but was still a nice burnished-bronze color. His hair was dark with a tinge of red; and was thick and very healthy looking, as though he were a man who'd been pampered his entire life. He sported a well-trimmed beard.

As I approached, his eyes met mine. Brown with a hint of green and framed by surprisingly long lashes, they spoke of a hunger for . . . what? Love? Knowledge? Happiness? Clearly, this wise man wasn't completely fulfilled.

He looked down at my feet. My face flushed hot as I realized the elaborate ruse he'd engineered in order to inspect them! I looked back at the pond with its crystal covering, then at Solomon, and said, "I thought that you'd take a more direct approach if you wanted to know something about me."

My bluntness surprised both of us. Solomon chuckled, perhaps because he realized I was a new sparring partner, one who would fearlessly match his wit.

I refused to bow to him, even though I knew that he and his court were waiting for this formality. I decided to curtsy as a way of saying hello while keeping my dignity. I wouldn't bow before any king but my own father! I fingered his necklace and stood my ground.

Solomon motioned for me to sit, and I just about fainted again when I saw the chair near his: It was my own throne! There was no doubt as I touched the familiar indent atop its right arm. My cushions and everything were arranged just as I had left the throne, locked tightly in a storage room so that no one could overthrow my position in my absence.

Fortunately, I caught myself and my passionate emotions before I could let on how surprised I was to see my throne in King Solomon's palace. Why give him the satisfaction that his little prank (however he'd pulled it off) had elicited my astonishment?

I felt a hand on my shoulder, and I saw Mother out of the corner of my right eye. I exhaled and sat on my throne without comment.

"My dear Queen Makeda," King Solomon began, perfectly enunciating my native Sabaean. "We weren't expecting you for several more months. Your journey must have been as remarkable as it was rapid. I look forward to hearing about it, and getting to know about you and your country in *direct* discussions."

"Yes, the trip *was* remarkable," I replied without acknowledging his remark, which was clearly a retort to my earlier chastisement about his using the pond to look at my feet instead of directly asking me about them. This man didn't miss—or refrain from commenting about—anything! Still, my instincts told me to stay quiet about my feet and most of my other personal information.

"We have some gifts for you and your kingdom," I said, signaling Tamrin to come forward. Tamrin bowed in deference to the king and gave me a sidelong look that said, *Why are you being so impertinent to the king?* I shrugged my shoulder just enough to convey to Tamrin, *I'm not sure.*

It was true. I *didn't* know why I felt so rebellious. I wasn't threatened by the king's arrogance or the opulence of his palace, since my own commonwealth was very prosperous and securely far away from Jerusalem. No, it was something more personal that I didn't quite understand, but still trusted.

Tamrin cleared his throat and read a scroll listing the gifts we'd brought the king, including the gold and silver that our country had in such abundance, spices, gemstones, camels, and lumber. Every now and then, Tamrin's Hebrew pronunciation wasn't clear, so Solomon's council would huddle and discuss the translations in loud whispers. I found the whole thing comical, which helped me relax.

Solomon and a very important-looking older man whom he introduced as his Chief of Council reciprocated with a very generous list of gifts for us. They also presented us with gold, silver, and camels so that our gifts basically canceled each other out!

After the formalities of the gift exchange, Solomon ceremoniously announced that it was noon and time for lunch. He beckoned for us to join him. I looked at Tamrin and whispered loudly, "But it's our worship time!"

Tamrin cleared his throat and motioned to one of Solomon's advisors. They spoke in hushed whispers, until the advisor nodded. Solomon, who'd watched the two men's discussion, nodded for the advisor to approach him. After the advisor explained about our afternoon worship, the king smiled at me.

"Ah, my good Queen of Sheba, please forgive my ignorance of your commonwealth's religious practices," he began. I started to reassure him, but Solomon kept talking: "My aides will escort you to a beautiful courtyard area where there is plenty of room for your worship, and we'll keep your lunch fresh and hot, awaiting the time when you are ready to eat." Solomon then extended his arms in a grand gesture that made me feel like applauding.

Our priests assembled an altar for the worship ceremony in the courtyard, complete with the portable statues, incense holders, and sun-ray obelisks that we'd used during our journey. As we bowed before each deity and chanted in response to the priests' prayers, I could feel Solomon's eyes watching us . . . or was I imagining it? I turned to look at the palace windows and saw a dark figure move. A chill went up my spine and my face flushed. Had he seen me looking at him?

After the ceremony, I was seated near King Solomon in the large dining room. Seven crystal chandeliers illuminated the golden silk cloth covering the long table. Servants darted about, seamlessly serving delicious hot vegetable and meat dishes from painted porcelain bowls.

I ate self-consciously, as I sensed Solomon watching me. Why did I get the feeling that he enjoyed my discomfort? I gripped the carved wooden arm of my padded chair. Suddenly I didn't feel hungry.

"Why don't we take a walk?" suggested Solomon.

How could I refuse him? As we stood, everyone stopped eating. The king motioned for them to continue, and we walked through a door near the courtyard where we'd held our worship ceremony. Two men whom I assumed were bodyguards trailed behind us, giving us privacy but always keeping us within view.

The palace garden was lavish with colorful, fragrant flowers spilling on top of each other. A series of connected ponds and waterfalls was home to swans and flamingos. Peacocks roamed the grassy lawns.

I searched for something to say. Finally, I remembered Tamrin's tales about King Solomon. "Tamrin says that you enjoy solving puzzles and riddles," I remarked without looking at him. I was definitely intimidated by his powerful presence.

"Riddles are good exercise for the mental muscles," Solomon replied, taking my hand with a surprisingly strong grip. My hand felt very petite in comparison to his big, masculine one. His right index finger sported a large golden ring. As we walked, I studied it with my peripheral vision. It was heavy looking and round and had a six-pointed star in its center encircled by four different-colored gemstones, with four Hebrew-looking letters at its base.

"My good friend the King of Tyre and I send each other riddles all of the time. Why? Do you have any you'd care to share?"

Actually, I didn't, but Mother promised that she'd help. I looked around for her and panicked that I'd now seem like a fool for bringing up the topic of riddles when I couldn't produce any.

"Ask him: 'What land has been covered with sunshine only one time in history?'"

Thank goodness you're here! I mentally chastised Mother for frightening me with her inopportune absence. I then repeated her words verbatim to King Solomon.

He squeezed my hand affectionately, and his eyes sparkled with more appreciation than they had for any of our expensive gifts. He stopped walking and closed his eyes, humming an indistinguishable tune.

"Wait a minute!" Mother practically yelled in my ear. "Solomon's getting answers and information from two men!"

What?! I thought. *What two men?*

"I'll check it out and get right back to you," she promised.

Mother, wait! I mentally called out. How would I even know if Solomon gave me the correct answer?

Solomon opened his eyes and smiled at me. My stomach tightened and I swallowed hard. "What a delightful riddle, my dear!" he said. "The answer is: *the Red Sea.* This location only saw sunshine on the one day when it parted for Moses and the Israelites to pass safely through on their exodus out of Egypt."

I scrambled for a reply but instead just nodded weakly. I remembered Tamrin talking about Moses receiving the Ten Commandments, but this story of the Red Sea parting was new to me. I smiled noncommittally at Solomon to buy time while waiting for Mother to rescue me.

"Okay, I'm back!" Mother said breathlessly in my ear. "What did I miss?"

Arghh! I thought as I mentally repeated Solomon's answer to Mother.

"He's absolutely correct!" I winced as Mother applauded in my ear.

"You are correct, King Solomon," I finally murmured.

Solomon looked in Mother's direction. Did he see her? "No he doesn't see me," Mother answered, "but he does hear at very high vibrational levels. Those two men I saw talking with Solomon are archangels."

Arch—what? I asked mentally while Solomon and I continued our walk, hand in hand. Every now and then, the king would stop to put his nose inside a flower blossom and inhale deeply. He'd then motion for me to do the same. The blooms of Jerusalem were very fragrant.

"Archangels are extremely high-level beings who bring pure wisdom and love to people," Mother explained. "Solomon works closely with two archangels named Michael and Metatron. They're the men I see with him who fed him the answer to the riddle."

When I asked Mother why I could see her but not Solomon's archangels, she said that Michael and Metatron's energy-frequency levels were considerably higher than her own. "We Jinn are very connected to Earth's beautiful dense energy," she said. "The archangels are more connected to the nonphysical elements of air and Spirit."

Well, that sort of made sense. Mother said that she had to increase the rate of her energy vibrations to connect with Solomon's archangels. She promised to help me do the same when the time was right.

"And do you have other riddles?" I was startled out of my mental conversation with Mother by Solomon's question.

Mother said, "Ask him, 'What is the item that helps sailors during a storm at sea, is the pride of the wealthy but the shame of the poor, and is a delight to the birds but a curse to the fish?'"

Now how was I supposed to remember all that long enough to ask Solomon? "Could you repeat the question more slowly?" I requested.

Mother fed it to me in smaller, bite-sized chunks. Solomon's expression was blissful! The more complex the riddle, the more ecstatic he seemed, and the louder he hummed. Yet I also knew of his secret archangel companions, who helped him solve these riddles. I wondered if *that* was the secret behind his wisdom.

Solomon relished each word of his answer. He said slowly, "The answer is *flax,* because it's woven into the sails of ships to guide them through storms, as well as into fine clothing for the wealthy and coarse rags for the poor. Birds love to eat flaxseeds, but fish are caught in nets made of woven flax."

Solomon answered with the glee of a young boy playing a sports game, without arrogance or the sense that he was trying to impress me. I studied his face: He was young, probably five years older than I was.

He had a youthful, mischievous spirit; yet he also possessed an old sage, almost wizardlike quality.

Solomon met my stare. I blushed with embarrassment at being caught gazing at his face. I realized that he was handsome—extremely so. His golden features were chiseled, and he radiated an aura of pure power.

"And the next riddle?" Solomon looked into my eyes as waves of energy passed between us. I tripped over a stick on the path and felt even more embarrassed and awkward.

"Pick up the stick," Mother directed.

Why? I asked her.

She explained that it was a tool for the next riddle. As Mother instructed, I handed the stick to Solomon and said, "Which part of this stick was nearest the trunk of the tree, and which was nearest the end of the branch?"

Solomon hummed while he inspected the stick, which was uniform in size so neither width nor narrowness signified the direction of growth. He then walked over to the beautiful pond in the middle of the garden. I followed him, curious as to what he'd do next.

He threw the stick into the pond, and although it floated at the surface, one end was lower than the other. He pointed to the end that was slightly submerged and said, "The part that's beneath the water was closest to the tree trunk, as it's accustomed to taking in the water

and delivering it to the other end of the branch that's elevated above the water."

I grimaced as Mother applauded and screeched into my right ear. "Mother!" I accidentally yelled aloud. Solomon looked at me inquisitively, and I covered my mistake by exclaiming, "Marvelous!"

Solomon pursed his lips in contemplation, raised his eyebrows, and then changed the subject. He was not only wise, but sensitive to other people's feelings. Points for Solomon!

"His archangels told him to be diplomatic and not to comment on how you screamed my name," Mother explained. "He listens to their guidance without question," she added, implying that I should do the same with *her* advice.

We neared the guest quarters, and Solomon walked me to the doorway of my chamber. He kissed my hand gallantly, and I curtsied to him. "Until tomorrow," he promised as soon as he ensured that I was in the good hands of one of the female attendants.

As I soaked in a flower-essence-infused bath, I looked at my feet. Maybe they weren't so bad after all!

CHAPTER 11

When I awoke the next morning, I knew that I'd been with *him* during the night. My lips were chapped and my nightdress was twisted, but I couldn't remember any details of our dreamtime rendevous.

Mother stood over my bed with folded arms. From her glare I could tell that she disapproved of my dream lover, but why would it matter, if it was just a dream? Too tired to discuss the matter with Mother, I smiled and motioned for Sarahil to begin our morning bathing and dressing rituals. I was happy to be wearing silk gowns, instead of the travel clothing that was utilitarian but unflattering and uncomfortably stiff.

After breakfast, King Solomon invited me into his private office. The decor was decidedly masculine, with dark wood paneling, wild-animal artwork, a musky smell, and thick rugs. Even his furniture seemed oversized and heavy.

Solomon sat on a chair at least a foot higher than mine, which meant I had to look up at him during our conversation. Since this felt like a power ploy on his part, I chose to stand. There—now *I* was the tallest one in the room!

When he looked up at me, his face transformed into that of a seven-year-old boy with impish eyes imploring a playmate to engage in fun antics. That's when I noticed that the king's desk was covered with carved wooden objects of varying geometric shapes. Some were simple cubes, while others had more sides than I could count.

"Queen Makeda, I'm curious to know about your religious beliefs and practices," he said. There were no subtleties at all when it came to this man! He was direct and to the point.

I explained that nature held great spiritual power; and that the sun and every planet, star, and moon worked in harmonious balance to give and support life. Our daily worship consisted of giving praise for these benevolent forces and asking that they continue to send sunshine, rain, moonlight, healthy crops and cattle, and other gifts.

"It's very clear that without the sun, rain, and moon, there would be no life, food, or goodness," I explained. "How could anyone think otherwise?"

Solomon's eyes crinkled and he hummed, obviously delighted to engage in a philosophical discussion.

"You're correct that the sun, moon, and rain are vital to maintaining our existence," he began (why did I get the feeling he was going to add a "however" to his sentence?). "However," he continued (aha!—I knew it!), "how do you imagine that the sun, moon, and rain clouds were created in the first place?" He leaned forward, eager to hear my reply.

Mother piped up: "Steady, Makeda. I'm right here." I exhaled with relief as she coached my reply: "Just say, 'The sun is the original energy from whence the moon, stars, and rain followed.'"

Solomon suppressed a chuckle as I repeated Mother's argument. I was insulted! He apologized, then asked in a condescending tone, as if he were talking to a child, "Do you imagine, then, that the sun has always been here?"

"Why, of course, yes," I replied without needing Mother's prompting.

"And what about the sky surrounding the sun? Has it always been here?"

Mother whispered, "Careful, Makeda. You're walking right into a trap of his logic."

But I was on a roll and didn't need her help. "The sun, sky, wind, rain, and all of the other holy components are eternal. They've always been here," I said matter-of-factly. Sheesh! These things were so obvious to me that I considered talking to *him* as if he were a child!

Solomon nodded, hummed, and caressed his beard. I wondered if he was listening to his archangel friends.

"Yes, he is," Mother hissed, "and I wish you'd listen to me!" I ignored her.

Finally, he replied, "What is the sky contained within?"

"Excuse me?" His question made no sense.

"Well, what is the container in which the sky rests?" he reworded the same query, still making no sense.

"For goodness' sake, Makeda!" exclaimed Mother. She said something about the eternal Universe, but I glazed over it. Besides, I wanted to win this argument on my own.

"The sky is not within a container. The sky *is* the container for everything else," I stated authoritatively.

"So where does the sky end?" Solomon immediately asked.

"It doesn't," I replied. Wow, this felt good. I must have absorbed some of this information from the priests' lectures!

"So the sky just extends endlessly," Solomon confirmed.

"Yes, that's correct." Well, well. The famous wise king was now learning from *me!*

"And the sky and the sun have always been there?"

"Yes, that's also correct," I replied.

"Careful!" Mother was now shaking my right shoulder. I wrenched away hard to release her grip, sending her flying across Solomon's room! *Oh Mother, I'm so sorry!*

She stood up and dusted herself off. I had to remind myself that Mother didn't have a physical body, so she was essentially unbreakable. Instead of returning to my side, she stood in between Solomon and me, with hands folded across her chest. She was done helping me, which was fine, since I didn't want or need her assistance anyway!

"And what is the sun god's name?" Solomon asked.

"Almaqah," I calmly responded, enjoying my new-found teaching role.

"And Almaqah's a real, live being with a soul and a personality?"

"Yes, he's the greatest power of them all!"

"And what are your parents' names?"

"My mother's name is Ismenie, and my father was known as Shar Habil. Why do you ask?"

"Because all living beings—including humans, animals, and even plants—have parents. Isn't that correct?"

"Yes, of course."

"And the name of Almaqah's parents?"

"Excuse me?"

"Well, you just told me that Almaqah is a real, live being and you agreed that all beings have parents. So who, or what, were Almaqah's parents?"

I looked at Mother, who gave me an *I told you so!* glance. I stared over Solomon's shoulders, straining to see his archangels, hoping they'd supply me with an answer.

I was stumped. Darn it, Mother was right! I'd walked right into Solomon's logic trap.

The king stood up, walked over to me, and put his hand in mine. He had the same glee in his eye that Tamrin had after a hunting expedition. He obviously enjoyed winning.

"Let me show you something," the king said cryptically, leading me down a dark corridor. It seemed like a back passageway that was purposely unlit and windowless. We turned left at the end of the hall and went down another passage. The sound of my shoes echoed against the marble floor and walls. I could hear Solomon's bodyguards shuffling behind us.

"Where are we going?" I finally had the presence of mind to ask.

"To the room where Almaqah's parents live!" he answered mysteriously.

When he held open the door for me, I winced as my eyes adjusted to the bright sunshine. He helped me climb into a white and gold chariot pulled by three large white horses. After riding for several minutes, the horses slowed as we neared a large mountain. Sounds of music and chanting were nearly drowned out by the horses' grunts as they strained to pull us uphill on a narrow, winding road. Two men dressed in white robes walked up a separate pathway. Their pace was slow, as if they were in a meditative trance.

"This is Mount Moriah," Solomon said. His voice startled me, as we'd both been silent during the ride. "It's a sacred place where God intervened as Abraham—the patriarch of our religion—was about to sacrifice his son Isaac. My father had an altar here that he'd fashioned from a threshing floor, which was used to separate the wheat from the chaff. God told him to build the temple on this location, to house the Ark of the Covenant."

The nearly noontime sunshine was reflected from a tall roof resembling stacked white boxes, successively growing smaller as they reached for the sky. Noontime! Horrified, I realized that it was almost the hour of worship! I considered asking Solomon to immediately return me to the palace, but then I decided that I could conduct private worship on this mountain.

We climbed out of the chariot and ascended white marble stairs. The chanting and music was louder now. Men wearing white shirts, pants, and cloth hats milled about the courtyard surrounding the staircase and temple building. A few men wore elaborate blue apronlike coverings over their white clothing, which made me feel as if they were esteemed or high priests. Others carried rocks and lumber along the side of the building. Several people held horns, drums, and stringed musical instruments.

To the left of the stairs a man was sanding an enormous circular bronze tub. When he looked in my direction, my face grew hot. *Why did he look so familiar?*

"Who is that?" I asked the king. We stopped on the third step to peer down at the man.

"Oh, that's Hiram, a brilliant architect from the land of Tyre. He's engineering the final touches on the temple, which includes this washing area for the high priests and the animals. Isn't it spectacular? I call it *The Molten Sea,* because it resembles ocean waves being carried upon the backs of oxen."

But I was focused on the man, not the basin he was polishing. Something about Hiram struck a chord deep within me, its music simultaneously discordant and pleasant. When he looked at me, I felt slightly faint.

Finally, we reached the top of the seemingly endless staircase, breathless from sprinting up the large steps. The chanting and music were overwhelmingly loud. Walking through a giant arched doorway flanked by golden pillars, we entered a wood-paneled lobby. Golden candlesticks illuminated the shiny wooden walls, which were intricately carved with images of winged beings, palm trees, flowers, and fruits. The entire room had a golden glow about it.

I had difficulty focusing as Solomon explained the significance of two enormous bronze pillars. My mind kept returning to the intriguing man sculpting *The Molten Sea*. "This is Boaz," the king announced, indicating the pillar on the left, "and this is Jachin," he said, patting the one on the right. He pointed to hieroglyphic carvings on the pillars and explained that they contained valuable information that Hiram had used in building the temple.

Where had I seen Hiram before? Solomon's voice faded into the background as I thought of every possible place I might have encountered the man from Tyre. Although I couldn't place it, I knew for certain that we'd previously met. I'd have to find a way to speak to him!

We walked past an enormous altar with a built-in fireplace. Solomon explained that it was used for something called "burnt offerings," which I really didn't want to know about. I shuddered at the thought of burning anything other than incense during a spiritual ceremony.

We slowed our pace as we neared a second room, which was separated by an elaborately embroidered purple, blue, and red curtain. "This is the sanctuary of the Holy of Holies, the room God instructed my father and me to build to house the sacred Ark of the Covenant."

I moved forward to peak behind the curtain, and the king and one of the priests grabbed me. "You can't go in there!" they both cried in unison. Their urgency surprised me.

Solomon inhaled sharply, obviously suppressing great emotion. "Only the purest of the high priests can enter that room," he said on the breath of his exhalation.

"Why?" I asked.

"Because the Ark of the Covenant radiates such strong frequencies that only people with matching energies can get near it. If they have even one ego-driven thought, the frequencies go out of sync, resulting in death."

"You mean people *die* when they get near the Ark?" I gasped. I hadn't quite believed Tamrin's earlier description of the Ark's lethal power.

"Watch this high priest entering the room." Solomon pointed. "See the white silken rope attached around his waist? That other priest will hold on to it. If the first priest should die while visiting the Ark, the other cannot go in and get him. To do so would mean risking his own life. Instead, he pulls the dead priest's body out."

As the high priest entered the room, he pulled back the curtain just enough so that I could see inside. The room was small—it was filled with a gilded box topped by two large carved figures with enormous wings that touched each wall. Moving lights seemed to emanate from the box. Yes, as I watched, the light was definitely glowing from within the box!

I turned to Solomon, who looked at me with amusement. He smirked and said, "It's true. The Ark really does glow."

"Where does the light come from?" I asked.

"From Almaqah's parents," the king explained. "That light is from Adonai, the One True God of Israel, Who created the sun, moon, stars, and everything else in nature . . . including you and me. The Ark of the Covenant is Adonai's *mishkan,* or dwelling place."

My eyes and head felt funny, as if a headache were coming on. I was obviously tired, because when I looked at Solomon again, he had three heads! Those on either side of his shoulders glowed with the same bluish white coloring as the golden box in the secret room. But wait—they weren't *Solomon's* heads! There were two distinct glowing men on each side of him.

Were they . . . ?

"Yes," Mother's familiar voice popped in.

Mother! Where on earth have you been? I mentally screeched.

"Leaving you alone so that you could do things on your own, as you requested," she said tensely.

So those two heads that I see next to Solomon . . . ? The vision was fading, and I needed to know what it meant.

"Those are Solomon's angels," Mother replied. "You're seeing the archangels Michael and Metatron."

The archangels looked just like the carved winged figures atop the Ark of the Covenant. I wondered if the word *archangel* shared a similar root with *Ark of the Covenant.*

Do the archangels see me? I gulped.

"Michael and Metatron see *everything,*" Mother said. "You see them now because the Ark's energy has opened your third eye."

My third what? I mentally inquired.

"The energy center between your two eyebrows. It allows you to see the nonphysical world, such as energy and angels."

But I can see you, Mother, and you're nonphysical.

"That's because our love has eternally joined us. All children and parents can contact each other through every dimension. You, Makeda, happen to trust your connection with me more than the average person, who thinks their feelings of a departed loved one's presence are merely imagination. So they ignore the real communications that the nonphysical world sends them."

Solomon looked at me with concern on his face. "It's almost time for your worship service," he said. "We'd better get you back to the palace courtyard." His thoughtfulness surprised me.

My forehead still felt uncomfortable. I could see colored lights around all of the people in the temple's lobby. Some had distastefully dark red ones, which made my stomach tighten. Others were surrounded by a beautiful blue, green, and purple radiance that stirred my heart. It seemed that the cooler colors were soothing, while the warm hues felt harsh. I also saw glowing figures around everyone.

Does everyone have archangels with them? I asked Mother.

"Everyone has *guardian* angels," she said, "but the archangels are willing to work with anybody who asks." I had a lot to learn.

The bright sunlight greeted the king and me as we walked through the arched door and descended the staircase, where the chariot awaited us at the bottom.

As I walked down the last step, I turned and saw that Hiram was looking at me. He smiled warmly and my heart melted. I so wanted to talk with him, but it was time to attend our worship. I returned his smile and nodded toward the chariot. Hiram signaled that he understood.

The priests were just beginning their chants and invocations when I arrived back at the palace. Tamrin and Sarahil looked sideways at me, and I smiled. I was getting very good at nonverbal communication!

During the noontime ceremony, my thoughts kept returning to the glowing Ark of the Covenant. I barely heard our worship service at all, bowing and chanting absentmindedly. Was it possible that there was a power greater than Almaqah and our other deities?

After the ceremony, Sarahil, Tamrin, and I walked to lunch together. I noticed a green glow around Tamrin. Sarahil's coloring was a tranquil pale blue, like the thinnest edges of the sky's horizon. I also saw glowing figures around both of them—they were angels!

This confused me. *Mother!* I called out in my mind. *I thought that only the Israelites had angels because of their beliefs in Adonai, but I can see them around Sarahil and Tamrin!*

"Every person has guardian angels, regardless of their spiritual path and faith," Mother told me.

How did Mother get so smart? *Do I have angels?* I marveled.

"Of course, darling," she spoke with a soothing voice, stroking my hair gently. "But you know what? I'm concerned about overwhelming you with too much information in one day. How about some lunch?" She rubbed her belly. Mother enjoyed eating vicariously through me.

I laughed, and then noticed Hiram standing near the palace door, staring at me. "Hiram!" I exclaimed, revealing my excitement more than I'd intended, considering we had not even met yet. I started toward him, but Mother, Sarahil, and Tamrin stopped me.

I struggled against Tamrin's grip as he led me away. I was furious at them for controlling me, even though I knew that they meant well. Hiram narrowed his eyes. My strong attraction to him confused me, but I resigned myself to having lunch with Tamrin and Sarahil. I was sure that Hiram and I would find some other way to meet.

CHAPTER 12

When I arose from my afternoon nap, I walked outside into the private garden courtyard next to my guest quarters to relax in the shade of a large, lovely oak tree. Sprays of fragrant flowers spilled onto the rocky waterfall beneath a wooden bridge.

A female attendant bowed to me and handed me a note. It was from King Solomon, written in perfect Sabaean, asking me to join him for a chariot ride to his favorite park. The attendant led me to the king, who was waiting in his beautiful white chariot. He was dressed in a long-sleeved white linen shirt and pants, with a royal-purple sash extending from his left shoulder to his right hip. The sash's color highlighted the deep purple jewels in the golden crown he always wore. Touching the top of my head, I realized that I was wearing mine as well.

Solomon gave me a pleasant smile as I entered the chariot. As he touched my right shoulder, I shivered with chill bumps. My stomach tightened.

"Everything's all right, darling," Mother reassured me as we rode through the arched entrance of Etan Park. The rolling hills of grass were dotted with orchids of every color and variety. Sprays of bright purple irises butted up against the park walls, which were covered in trailing pink roses.

Solomon led me to a grassy spot, where he laid out a thick woven tapestry. I started to relax, and we both reclined on our elbows to gaze at the pillowy white clouds. Rustling movement in the tree overhead caught my attention as a bird emerged from the thick leaves. *"Oop! Oop! Oop!"* it called.

"Hoopoe!" Solomon greeted the bird in a singsongy voice. The king held out his right index finger and the bird landed on top of his ring. He bent his head and seemed to listen to the bird even though I could only hear throaty chirping sounds. Solomon nodded and said, "Hmm." Could he actually be communicating with the bird?

"Hoopoe says that it's good to see you again," the king informed me. In response to my raised eyebrows, he explained, "He was the one who originally told me about you."

Okay, I guess if I could talk to my invisible mother, then it was also possible to talk with birds. I asked Solomon to continue.

"Hoopoe spent time with you and Tamrin in your palace courtyard," he explained.

That was true! There *was* a bird in our courtyard for quite a few days. Could this possibly be the same one?

Solomon raised his hand and the bird returned to the tree above us. The king looked at me with a serious expression.

"Hoopoe was on a very important assignment," the king continued. "You see, I'd asked him to find a truly sincere person for me. I don't know what your experience has been as royalty, but I've had difficulties with people always wanting something from me. I've only had one or two true friendships with people who like me for who I am and not for what I can do for them. Even my own brother tried to kill me in order to inherit my crown."

I nodded in understanding. The only companions I had were Tamrin and Sarahil. Well, Mother was my friend, but she was in a whole other category! Like King Solomon, I'd met my share of people who pretended to be friends and then used me for their own personal gain.

Solomon held my hands to his chest and looked into my eyes. "Queen Makeda, *you* are the person I've been looking for. You're sincere and entirely yourself. You want nothing from me, but are instead refreshingly generous with your gifts and the time you give me—so I was thanking the hoopoe for finding you, and for delivering my invitation to you."

The invitation! I snatched back my hand and stood upright. My voice trembled as I asked Solomon how he could send such a threatening message to me.

"My dear, I don't know what threats you're referring to," the king said, puzzled.

"Tamrin and my High Council all read your invitation. You threatened to harm me and my commonwealth if I didn't come to Israel to pay homage to you!" I was angry all over again upon recalling the very rude scroll.

"Oh, my beautiful Makeda." Solomon was so close that I could feel his warm breath on my face. "I would never threaten anyone, especially my most esteemed Queen of Sheba. There's obviously been a mistake in the translation from Hebrew to Sabaean! I have a copy of the invitation in my office, and I'll personally show it to you."

"Well, I don't read Hebrew," I said. Something made me trust his words, and I relaxed again. I wondered, though, how my most trusted advisors could have all misread Solomon's invitation.

"It happens all the time," said Mother. "Hebrew words are easily misread and misunderstood."

What are you doing here, Mother?! I mentally chastised her for invading my privacy.

"I just popped in and now I'm leaving!" she assured me.

As I watched Mother fade from view, I became aware that Solomon was speaking. "Thanks to my father's legacy, my reputation as a wordsmith has become so legendary that people often gossip about me and mistranslate my words. I really don't mind what people say, unless they put cruel words into my mouth, because that's just not who I am!

"The worst example was when I recently told some young parents that they needed to guide their son as a shepherd does his flock. I used the metaphor of raising their son with a *shebet* to avoid spoiling him. Well, a group of people mistranslated the Hebrew word *shebet*—which means 'shepherd's crook' or an instrument to guide sheep—and they started saying that I told the parents to use a 'rod' on the child. I'm horrified to learn that people are spanking their children because they're misquoting me as saying, 'Spare the rod and spoil the child!'" Solomon shuddered, and his eyes filled with tears.

I shared with him how my own life as a princess, and now a queen, had taught me the dark side of being constantly on public display. Like Solomon, I'd also heard stories told about me that had no basis in truth.

Solomon revealed that he was drawn to me because we had so much in common. He held my hands and said, "On top of our common background, I discover that you're the true and sincere person I've been seeking, *and* that you're also as beautiful on the outside as you are on the inside. Your heart is unspoiled, your mind is sharp, and your wit is as colorful as these garden flowers.

"Who can find a virtuous wife? For her worth is far above rubies. Her husband can trust her, and she will greatly enrich his life." Solomon knelt before me and softly said, "Makeda, would you do me the honor of becoming my wife and serving as my queen of Israel?"

I looked at his handsome, chiseled face. His eyes appeared tired beyond his years, yet behind this weary wisdom was an insecure little boy who just wanted to be loved. I held him in an embrace of maternal friendship and caring. I could really relate to Solomon's loneliness. Perhaps marrying him would be a solution for both of us.

But wait! What about the vows I took on my coronation day? How could I explain to Solomon that I'd pledged my chastity to Almaqah, and that—while deeply honored by his proposal—I wasn't allowed to marry or be with any man other than the sun god?

"You give it some thought then, Makeda," Solomon advised, patting my hand. "I know what it feels like to be pressured into making a decision, and I don't want to do that to you. Besides, it's getting late and we need to return to the palace."

A blazing orange and pink sunset filled the sky as we rode back. Solomon looked at me deeply as we arrived at my guest quarters. "Until tomorrow." He bowed, gently kissing my right hand. I could feel Solomon's need for companionship as he rode off alone in his chariot with his bodyguards following in a second one.

As I crossed the courtyard, I saw a figure walking toward me. I assumed that it was a female attendant coming to greet me and escort me to my room. I planned to ask for a bath after my long afternoon in the park.

"*Ahalan,*" said a hushed male voice. I stopped and held my breath. This was no attendant, but a man, and men weren't allowed in the guest courtyard after sundown. I was about to protest his presence when I realized that it was Hiram! (I'd later learn that *Ahalan* meant "hello" in Phoenician, which was the architect's native language.)

Hiram put his hand on my shoulder and walked me to the courtyard gate. The smell of sandalwood and sweat drifted from his shirt to my nose as he brought me to a small, unpainted single-horse chariot. I worried that someone would notice us as we climbed into it.

I watched Hiram's face in the moonlight as we rode wordlessly together. His skin looked toughened from hard work done outdoors, and his mouth moved slightly as if he were talking to himself. His browridge was etched with lines, probably from squinting while sculpting outside in bright sunlight.

He looked at me, caught my glance, and smiled so widely that his forehead smoothed and his eyes looked youthful. My heart quivered with pleasant, unfamiliar feelings.

Up ahead of us moonlight danced upon a tall structure. As we drew near, I recognized it as the temple's towering layered rooftop. *Hiram is taking me to the temple!* I realized excitedly.

We bypassed the front entrance where Solomon had taken me and went around the side to an area that was still under construction. Chairs sat in a semicircle in front of a pile of gigantic stones. We walked along a path into the temple's pristine lobby, where candles glowed from their golden holders. Hiram pulled me into a doorway as footsteps approached and signaled for me to stay quiet until a man passed by. We obviously weren't supposed to be in the temple!

After looking down the hallway to ensure that we were alone, we padded softly through the lobby toward the colorful curtain of the Holy of Holies. Hiram held it open and motioned for me to enter. I gulped, looking at the glowing Ark of the Covenant, which seemed to call to me. Oh, how I wanted to stand by its side! But what punishment awaited me if I got caught in the forbidden room? And hadn't I learned that if someone wasn't pure enough to stand near the Ark, they were instantly struck dead?

My breath and heartbeat caught in my throat until Hiram ended my hesitation by pushing me through the curtain. I trusted that he, one of the architects of the temple, knew what he was doing.

The room was surprisingly small. The wings of the two carved angels on top of the Ark and the poles on either side of its box touched the walls. Since there was no place to sit, I knelt by the box. A high-pitched buzzing sound, like thousands of voices singing far away, emanated from inside. My head began to hurt, and I saw glowing purple light swirl around the room.

Something touched my forehead and I jumped. "Hiram?" I called out quietly, and opened my eyes to see a man dressed in white standing before me. I backed away, frightened of being punished for trespassing in this holy place.

But the man smiled and said, "Do not be afraid, Makeda." He seemed to know who I was! And he looked familiar to me as well. Although the man was three-dimensional, I realized that he was translucent and I could see the Ark's box through his body. I felt afraid—maybe I was too impure to be there and I was dying!

I began backing out of the room, praying to find Hiram before it was too late. The man came toward me and held out his hand. A swirling geometric pattern glowing red, purple, and green danced above his outstretched palm. I recognized part of the intersecting triangles from Solomon's ring. The pattern pulsated and produced high-pitched ringing sounds that I found both soothing and uncomfortable.

"Makeda, this is your destiny," the man said. "You are exactly where you need to be, and you are entirely safe and protected."

"W-who are you?" I stammered.

"They call me Metatron." He bowed.

"The archangel?" I asked. "The one who helps King Solomon?"

"Yes, I help many people as part of my global mission," he replied. Metatron wasn't standing in front of me, but he wasn't floating either. He seemed to grow brighter, dimmer, opaque, and transparent as a function of the Ark's glowing and fading light. *Was he fueled by the Ark?* I wondered.

"Everything is fueled by Adonai," Metatron said in answer to my unspoken question. Oh, I'd have to watch my thoughts around Metatron, just as I did around Mother!

"But I don't believe in Adonai, or whatever you call this energy," I said. "I believe in Almaqah, the sun god who's the bringer of life."

"It does not matter whether you believe in Adonai, because Adonai exists with or without our belief." Metatron smiled. So this was where Solomon got his dry wit! "Adonai is the life-force spirit that animates you, me, Solomon, and every living being, including the sun."

"Well, I don't really understand this whole concept of Adonai," I said, rubbing my temples to stop the buzzing, tingling sensations. "Where is Adonai?"

"Everywhere," replied Metatron. "Every part of physical and nonphysical life is fueled by Adonai."

"Well, what *is* Adonai?" I truly didn't understand.

"Adonai is the mother and father of everything you see, touch, feel, and experience. Adonai is the giver of life, as well as life itself."

"Including the bad and painful parts of life?" I asked.

"There are no bad or painful parts of life within Adonai, only within the dream that humans have created."

Now I was really confused. "The dream?"

"The legends about the fall of humanity allude to this dream. It occurred when the human mind desired complete autonomy, apart from Adonai's will. It wanted to experiment with being a creator, and this wish to separate from Adonai created the dream in which all humans now find themselves. You believe that you are disconnected from each other and from Adonai, when in fact that would be impossible. The only way to be apart from Adonai's will is to imagine it, which is this very realistic dream that all humans find themselves living in."

"A dream that we're separate from Adonai," I reiterated.

"Yes," Metatron confirmed. "And because Adonai is the light and love that fuels your soul and spirit, you are completely connected to your power source."

"And we're dreaming that we're having problems and pain?" I inquired with trepidation, not quite sure if I was understanding the concept.

"Yes, that is exactly right!" Metatron congratulated me. "Every person holds great Divine wisdom because all human minds are completely connected to Adonai's infinite knowledge. You, like everyone, have access to all information and answers."

"I do?"

"Yes, of course," answered Metatron.

"How do I access this wisdom?"

"You ask Adonai questions."

"How?"

"You can do so aloud, silently, through song, or in any way you like."

"And Adonai will answer my questions?"

"Yes," replied Metatron. "Adonai is an energy that responds to other energies. Your questions trigger matching answers, like a lock and a key. Everything is mathematically precise."

He held his right hand in front of him. Out of his upward-facing palm colorful lights twirled in a fast spinning motion. The lights began to solidify into particles, and then a definite shape with intersecting triangles:

"Hear that sound?" Metatron asked. The spinning motion of the geometric shape was like hundreds of voices all singing *"Ahhhh."*

"That's beautiful and very soothing," I replied. "What is it?"

"The sound of creation," Metatron said. "When you receive answers and guidance from Adonai, you have an 'Aha!' moment. This is a true connection to Universal Wisdom, when understanding flashes its light across your entire being."

"The sound I'm hearing is Adonai?" Although Metatron's words intuitively made sense, I wanted to make sure I understood him.

"You are correct, Makeda. It is an intuitive under-standing that bypasses logic and reason," Metatron said. "Every culture intuitively uses the 'Ah' sound in

the name they choose for their Creator God. Here in Israel, the term *Adonai* is used. Other cultures call the Creator by the name God, Yahweh, Brahma, Ra, Baal, and so forth. The common denominator is *Ah.*"

"Why does this geometric shape make the sound of creation?" I asked, still not understanding.

"Because every creation is based upon geometric shapes and figures. All physical matter is a combination of five basic forms." Metatron's geometric lights began twirling and slowed down to form five distinct spinning shapes that hovered in front of me.

Tetrahedron

Cube

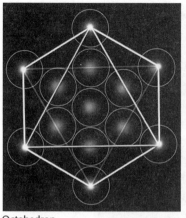

Octahedron

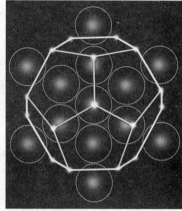

Dodecahedron

Icosahedron

He pointed to the first one and said, "This is a triangle or tetrahedron. This second shape is a cube, followed by an octahedron, then a dodecahedron, and finally an icosahedron.

"This," he said, sweeping his hands across the five spinning shapes, "is what creation is based upon. When you add them together like this"—all of the shapes merged to form the swirling vortex that Metatron had originally shown to me—"then they make the sound of creation, which is *'Ahhhh.'* Some people refer to this combined shape as my, or rather, *Metatron's,* cube."

It was difficult for me to concentrate on the archangel's words because something kept banging against my chin. I looked down to see my dragon bloodstone necklace floating in front of me! I pushed the stone back beneath my gown, yet it still drifted upward. "What in the world?!" I exclaimed when the necklace wouldn't stay flat.

Metatron pointed at a pendant of his own that was also floating and said, "The music of the spheres."

When I responded to this explanation with a blank stare, Metatron continued sweetly: "The music of the spheres is the energy that supports every star and planet in the heavens. As you look into the evening sky, each planet is arranged with Adonai's signature, which is the mathematical value 1.618034. Some call this number 'golden' because it is the most valuable key to the Universe. The ratios of the planets' cycles around the sun and their distance from each other in

relationship to it all average 1.618034. Seashells, pinecones, and even vegetables all grow in the same circular ratio as the planets' orbits, which is magnetically influenced by the music of the spheres.

"The quartz basis of all planets is derived from a binary, or dual, mathematical formula that resonates to the sound of creation. So it is with your necklace and my pendant, as they both have a quartz basis. The quartz amplifies all energy it comes into contact with in a process called *piezoelectricity*."

Suddenly the room was filled with thousands of tiny specks floating in the air. I thought that a windstorm had blown in sand particles, but as I looked closer, I realized that the dots were colorful shapes, much smaller than any sand grain I'd ever seen. The dots flew in circular orbits, next to each other and perfectly spaced apart from one another. I reached out to touch them, but my hand passed right through them without interrupting their perfect orbits.

Metatron chuckled fondly. I loved his sense of humor and never felt that he was laughing at me. Instead, he took a childlike delight in educating me.

"This temple was built by the music of the spheres!" Metatron exclaimed, almost like an announcement.

"What do you mean?" I couldn't understand how music could create a physical building.

"You will find out very soon . . ." Metatron answered, escorting me out of the Holy of Holies. Hiram, who apparently didn't see the archangel, grabbed my arm so that we wouldn't be observed by the guards or priests.

CHAPTER 13

The chariot slowed and finally stopped at the side of the road. Hiram reached for my hand to help me step down. The moonlight illuminated his wide eyes, which explored mine with an urgency I didn't understand. My breath deepened as Hiram put his hand behind my head and pulled me closer. I breathed in his cologne, which smelled like sandalwood.

Sandalwood! I sharply inhaled as I realized how I knew Hiram. "You're *him!*" I said, pulling back to look at his face. Hiram didn't understand my words since we didn't share a common tongue, yet our bodies spoke the same language.

Hiram smiled and gently pulled my head toward his. The man from my dreams was solid and three-dimensional, and any resistance that I had vanished as I yielded to the moment. Finally, I was able to kiss his lips while awake, merging into his sandalwood scent and strong, burly arms. Hiram was a romantic gentleman, limiting his affections to kissing and never asking for more. We embraced in the moonlight for hours without speaking, until the edges of sunlight crept over the mountains.

Finally I pulled away and motioned for Hiram to return me to the palace before anyone noticed my absence (if they hadn't already!). I exited his chariot just outside the private courtyard. The palace guard was slumped over, asleep on his late-night shift. As I hurried through the gate, I heard a rustling noise inside the courtyard and saw a dark figure move hurriedly to my right. When I turned, the figure was gone.

Solomon sent for me the next morning. After breakfast, I walked through the palace corridors to enjoy the elaborate architectural structure. Metatron's teachings inspired me to look at buildings in an entirely new way! I noticed the precise carvings of pillars, spirals, and sconces.

I was so busy gazing up at the ceiling that I bumped straight into Solomon as he turned the corner from his chambers. "Well, good morning!" he greeted me, his eyes smiling.

I gulped, feeling guilty, as if I'd cheated on him last night with Hiram. I quickly checked this emotion by reminding myself that I had no commitment or obligation to the king. Besides, Hiram and I had merely kissed, nothing more.

"Good morning." I smiled in return and followed Solomon into his office. I flipped through some drawings that were sitting on the low table by his sofa, wondering what to say. So much had changed after the previous night's encounters with Metatron and Hiram!

Metatron! I looked up at Solomon's left shoulder and—although he wasn't as clearly visible as the night before when I was fueled by the Ark's energy—I could see a wispy, cloudy presence and somehow I knew that it was him. I wondered if the archangel would betray my secrets to the king.

"How was your evening, Queen Makeda?" Solomon stood up and looked out his window. My heart stopped. Did he know about last night? Should I just go ahead and confess?

I gulped and said, "It was fine, thank you." Best to be neutral, I decided.

"I was thinking that maybe you'd like to return to the temple?" Solomon asked coyly. I wondered if he could see my hands shaking.

I nodded so my voice wouldn't betray me. My pulse pounded as loudly as drumbeats in my head. Why did I feel so guilty when I'd really done nothing wrong?

"Because Solomon is your destiny," I heard Mother whisper into my ear. *Mother! Oh no, not right now!*

The sparkling lights next to Solomon's left shoulder grew brighter and seemed to come toward me. I leaned back as the illuminated cloud headed in my direction! It looked like a hazy sunset, flowing with amber, orange, and blue. As I breathed, my head felt dizzy and I was faint. Wind blew hard against my skin and hair, and I squeezed my eyes shut.

Solomon's hand held mine, and its strong assurance calmed me. I opened my eyes and saw that he and I were no longer in his room, but sitting on a huge green tapestry carpet. For some reason, I wasn't alarmed by the fact that we were floating across the sky, completely suspended above the desert landscape. Something about Solomon's calm demeanor was contagious. I didn't dare move for fear of tipping the carpet. The wind roared so loudly that I couldn't ask Solomon what we were doing or even hear if Mother was with me.

I saw the now-familiar temple roof up ahead of us. As we zoomed down to it, I cringed as we flew straight toward the wall.

"Are you trying to kill us?!" I screamed, grabbing Solomon and preparing to jump off of the carpet.

Solomon was oblivious to my screams and the fast-approaching wall. He looked straight ahead with a blissful, meditative expression. I silently prayed to Almaqah, asking that he spare us from a painful death. We were now inches from the wall, and I closed my eyes, bracing myself for the impact.

But instead of crashing, we passed straight through it! I brushed my hands across my shoulders to confirm that I was still alive and intact.

Now inside, we hovered so close to the temple's ceiling that I had to bend to avoid hitting my head. *What's going on?* I thought as my hand passed through a carved spiraled sconce I tried to touch on the ceiling.

Solomon turned to me. Archangel Metatron stood next to his left shoulder, and another figure was beside his right one. The second figure was radiant, like Metatron, as if light were inside his head and streamed out of every pore. Even his hair glowed with a liquid golden light. He wore a royal-purple cape that I initially thought was made of satin, but upon closer inspection, I saw that it consisted of fluid purple radiance. He held a beam of golden light in his right hand that looked like a sword but obviously wasn't, since it wasn't solid or metal.

"Look down there," Solomon said to me, pointing to the temple lobby below. A woman and man were scurrying toward the curtain separating the area from the Holy of Holies. I watched the man pull back the curtain and point toward the Ark of the Covenant. The woman was animated, discussing something.

I gasped. *The woman was me!*

Solomon's face drew closer to mine as he watched me watch myself. How was this possible: to be up on the carpet with Solomon while I was also simultaneously down in the lobby? I couldn't take my eyes off of the scene.

I realized that I was seeing myself and Hiram the night before. Horrified that my secret was so openly exposed, I felt hot tears stream down my cheeks.

"The reverberations and echoes of everything we do remain trapped within the walls of buildings," Solomon said. "Especially when we hold guilt for our actions. The guilt you've been feeling and your fears that your secret would be discovered have sent out signals that others can sense. We've got to clean the temple of these lower energies—now!"

The figure next to Solomon's right shoulder raised his light beam. Purple rays streamed out of it, pouring down into the temple lobby and onto Hiram and me below. The light moved in a tight circular motion like a small tornado, suctioning a dark and murky substance that looked just like rain clouds from Hiram and me and out of the temple.

"What was that?" I asked Solomon when it was all over.

"Queen Makeda, please meet the archangel Michael." We nodded to each other, and Solomon continued: "Michael ensures that the physical world is cleared of lower energies such as fear, guilt, and greed."

"Wow, that's a big job!" I remarked. Michael smiled at me, and I felt my heart tingle with warmth, just as if I were outside in the sunshine. I closed my eyes to savor the sensation.

"The temple was Adonai's decree, given to my father, King David," Solomon said.

When I opened my eyes, we were back in Solomon's office! My head was spinning, and I walked to the window for fresh air. Archangel Michael followed and wordlessly waved his hand over me. My head immediately cleared.

"My dear, are you feeling okay?" Solomon asked, bringing me some water and helping me to the sofa, where he sat beside me.

I drank the water and stammered that I felt better. Solomon put his arm behind my head on the back of the sofa and said, "Adonai gave very explicit instructions to my father about the dimensions and purpose of the temple. Yet he wasn't to build it because of his involvement with wars. The legacy that my father left me, and the reason why I inherited his crown, was to orchestrate the building of Adonai's Temple on Mount Moriah."

Solomon looked at me intently and said, "I couldn't build it alone. Obviously, I needed help, so my good friend the King of Tyre sent me loads of cedarwood, crystals, and gold leafing. He also lent me his chief architect to oversee the temple's construction. That architect is your friend Hiram Abiff."

I blushed and looked down. Could I have no secrets?

"Hiram is a master mason and the finest construction contractor in the land," Solomon continued. "He knows the secrets of architecture and how to put them into motion. I hired Hiram because he understands that Adonai is the grand Architect of the Universe. Hiram is a good man, but he has a problem."

"What's that?" I was concerned.

"He doesn't know how to delegate. His workers all want to apprentice and acquire the knowledge of his trade, but Hiram feels that they're not ready to learn the inner secrets of architecture and masonry. That's why he's always working on the temple single-handedly."

This didn't sound like too much of a problem to me until Solomon explained that Hiram's workers were growing increasingly jealous and frustrated. "They came to Jerusalem expecting to be Hiram's apprentices. Instead, they're told to carry rocks to the construction area," Solomon explained. "Archangel Michael has been working overtime to lift and clear the jealous energy from the workers, but every day their frustration grows as Hiram refuses to teach them the trade. I'm concerned for the temple's energy, and I'm also concerned about Hiram's safety."

"His safety?" I was alarmed.

"Yes, I have reason to believe that Hiram's men are conspiring against him," Solomon replied. "But please don't worry." Solomon gently took my right hand. Bringing it to his lips, he sweetly kissed and stroked it.

"Have you given any more thought to our discussion last night?" He looked at me.

I considered pretending not to understand his question, but something within me urged me to be honest with the king. "Of course I've thought about it," I said, carefully choosing my words.

Solomon's kisses inched their way up my arm, until his lips were brushing my neck and chin. If only I were attracted to him! We shared so much in common; and he was so handsome, wise, and good-hearted. But— I looked Solomon in the eyes—he wasn't Hiram. How could I reject him and possibly cause heartache and bad feelings?

"I'm married to Almaqah," I finally said. It was, after all, the truth (if not the *whole* truth). "My commonwealth's laws state that I must remain an unwed virgin."

Solomon pulled away. "It's Hiram, isn't it?" He peered at me through narrowed eyes, and I gulped. Metatron and Michael both shrugged, indicating that they hadn't said anything to Solomon. For some reason, I suddenly felt afraid for Hiram.

"Well, it's time for your worship ceremony anyway," Solomon said, standing up and offering his hand to help me off of the couch. *He has so much class to be nice to me, despite my rejection of his affections,* I thought as we walked toward the courtyard.

I could see Hiram watching me during our noontime worship ceremony. I smiled and waved my hand so that only he could see.

I must warn him! I realized.

CHAPTER 14

After our ceremony, I told Sarahil and Tamrin that I was going to take a nap. I kept walking, though, right past my room and through the courtyard door, out to the area where chariots normally waited. Since it was lunchtime and no one was expecting a ride, there were none present. I looked around and worried whether I was emitting guilt, which would enable Solomon and his angels to see me. Then I remembered that guilt only gets trapped when it's inside buildings. I did feel bad about lying to Sarahil and Tamrin, but this was eclipsed by my desire to be with Hiram.

I had no idea which direction to walk in. Fortunately, everyone was eating lunch, so I was totally alone. The hot sun radiated above the top of my head, and its rays reflected upward from the stone pavers lining the street. I looked up, hoping for a cloud covering, when I realized that the sun could actually help me!

It had been weeks since I'd channeled the solar rays and successfully teleported our caravan to Jerusalem. I wondered if I was out of practice, but nonetheless I decided to give it a try. I cupped my hands while imagining myself with Hiram at that moment. I visualized this scene floating directly in front of my solar plexus, just as Mother had taught me. I then inhaled the sun's rays and pictured myself exhaling this energy out into the vision of Hiram and myself.

I kept inhaling and exhaling, filling the romantic vision with increasing light. My heart was full and warm, as if Hiram were holding me closely. I could smell his sandalwood scent; taste his lips; and feel his strong, muscular arms. It felt and sounded so real, since I was using all of my senses to transform my desires into reality. My arms were covered with goose bumps as I felt Hiram lightly run his fingers up and down them.

I reached out to stroke his hand and realized that this was no vision—it *was* Hiram! The Statement of Empowerment had worked once again, and our lips celebrated this reunion. I looked around to make sure that no one would see us and found that I'd been transported away from the palace and we were standing behind *The Molten Sea*, the bronze tub that Hiram was creating.

I worried about returning to the temple grounds so soon after Solomon's discovery of our previous tryst, but I reassured myself that we were outdoors, so we weren't contaminating the building with guilt. Besides, there was something metaphysical about meeting the man who'd come into my dreams so many times. I had to discover the meaning behind those dreams and my feelings, along with the reason why Mother was so adamantly opposed to our relationship.

Hiram helped me climb up a ladder propped against the side of *The Molten Sea*. He followed me inside the basin, the interior of which was just as gorgeous and ornate as its exterior. Every sound we made echoed and vibrated, so we sat silently together, holding one another.

I felt so happy with Hiram . . . so peaceful and safe, as if I'd known him forever, although I knew nothing about him since we spoke different languages and couldn't communicate. The basis of our relationship was a strong electric magnetism that drew us together, both in dreams and in waking time.

My stomach tightened with a pang, and I realized that as content as I felt, unease also clamored within me. When I focused on my stomach and asked it to tell me its feelings, I received the answer that my relationship with Hiram felt temporary and tentative. This realization caused me more anxiety, so I performed a mental trick that Mother had shown me: I imagined myself in the future to see if Hiram was by my side. I looked at my royal duties and my home life, yet no matter how much I searched, I couldn't see or feel him in my future. Hot tears filled my eyes at the unfairness of it all. How could I be so privileged in terms of wealth and power, yet be so unfulfilled in my love life?

Hiram must have sensed my discord, because he held me tighter. My stomach fluttered with excitement, and I swallowed hard as he stroked my back in a soothing way. In his arms, I felt so safe and life seemed simple. I just wanted to stay like that forever.

Fortunately, Hiram felt the same way about me, and over the course of the days that followed, we met every day and most evenings. I used Statements of Empowerment and the rays of the sun and the moon to cloak Hiram and myself from others' prying eyes.

Since we didn't know each other's language, we used drawings and hand signals to communicate. Hiram's knowledge of architecture was boundless; and he pointed out geometric shapes in everyday objects of nature, such as the circular rings in tree stumps, the perfect patterns of palm fronds, and the thirteen rectangles on tortoise shells.

I watched Hiram, shirtless with bronzed bulging biceps, work on *The Molten Sea* sculpture using a torch and sanding planes to finish the details. I observed him bring its twelve bronze oxen to life with his artistry. I admired how much care and attention Hiram gave each animal's eyes, making sure they held just the right level of humble, loving expressiveness.

Although he had apprentice helpers available, Hiram always chose to work alone. Without speaking, he managed to convey to me that his assistants just weren't ready for the esoteric information of sacred masonry. I watched the apprentices shrink every time Hiram told them he didn't need their help. Three of them seemed particularly insistent in their desire to work with Hiram. In fact, their intensity frightened me!

Hiram was ready to put the final touches on *The Molten Sea,* and he prepared a giant ring, into which he planned to pour molten bronze to create a band of cast-metal lilies around the top of the basin.

His artistry was particularly meticulous as he carved the casting mold for the flower ring. Sometimes he became so engrossed in this work that he seemed to forget I was there, yet if I began to make motions to return to the palace, he would always wake from his artistic trance and urge me to stay.

One such evening, as much as I wanted to remain with Hiram and watch him pour his liquid lilies, I felt tired, so I kissed him and cupped the full moon's rays to transport myself to my bedroom. I fell deeply asleep until I was awakened in the middle of the night by men yelling and running outside the courtyard. I could hear them hitching horses to chariots, followed by the unmistakable sound of hooves galloping away. I said quick prayers to Almaqah and Athtar to protect the men and their horses and to watch over whatever the emergency situation was. Then I fell back asleep.

Hiram came into my dreams that night. I ran to him for our embrace, but his arms were limp and his face looked pale. Startled, I asked him what was wrong. "I'm so sorry, Makeda," was all he said in perfect Sabaean, and then he disappeared.

I sat straight up in bed, my heart thumping loudly. Something was wrong—I knew it! I slipped on a long dress and headed out the door. My every instinct drew me to the temple and Hiram.

CHAPTER 15

Too shaken to effectively teleport myself to the temple, I shouted for a passing chariot to give me a ride. It stopped long enough for me to jump on, and within minutes we were at the foothills of Mount Moriah, where dozens of other chariots were parked. Men with lighted torches illuminated the area near *The Molten Sea*. Three men with their hands tied behind their backs were forcibly led away. As I neared the bronze basin, I saw four small fires smoldering near its base. Liquid bronze was splattered across one of Hiram's masterfully sculpted oxen.

I recognized the back of Tamrin's head as I drew closer. He and the other men were looking down at a river of liquid bronze on the ground. Hiram's lily-flower mold lay broken on the ground, and a man was sprawled in the middle of the metallic stream. His face and clothing were blackened, as if he'd been caught in the fire.

Tamrin saw me and put his hand out, barking, "Queen Balkis, stop!" as I moved toward the man. That's when I recognized the charred figure lying on the ground as Hiram.

"No!" I screamed, running to him. Tamrin and the other men barred my way and pulled me, struggling, back into the surrounding crowd.

"The liquid bronze and fires are too dangerous, Queen Balkis," Tamrin whispered loudly to me. "We don't want you killed, too."

Killed? Hiram's dead? I ran away, sobbing, up the temple staircase, turning briefly to look at the scene as I neared the two pillars at the top. A large flash of moonlight shone off the top of *The Molten Sea*, and carved lilies appeared around the rim as if by magic. I looked at the moon and saw Hiram's smiling face beaming at me.

"Hiram!" I cried, running to the Holy of Holies room. Maybe the Ark of the Covenant would comfort me and provide some answers as to why this craziness was happening. Perhaps it could even heal and revive poor Hiram!

I pushed back the curtains and stepped over the golden chain draped in front of the doorway. The room was dark except for the glowing light above the Ark's box between the two carved angels. A high-pitched whirling sound in perfect synchronization with the glowing light gave the room an eerie mood. A loud rumbling groan startled me, and I stepped back quickly as the box began jerking up and down like a bucking donkey.

A thick cloud of energy enfolded me, slowing my motions so that I couldn't escape the Ark's overwhelming groans. I fell to the floor, weakened by the thick energy around me, as if I were being held under deep water and couldn't breathe. The lights and sounds dimmed, and I wondered if I were dying.

I felt something around my legs, and I regained consciousness long enough to notice that I was being dragged along the floor.

"That was close!" a male voice said. I opened my eyes to see four men peering over me. I tried to get up, but my throbbing head forced me back into a horizontal position. "Just take it easy, Queen Makeda," said the same man, whom I now recognized as Tamrin.

I groaned and gratefully accepted the cup of water someone thrust into my hands. Slowly, I was pulled into a seated position. I put my head between my legs to keep from blacking out again. Someone rubbed my back, and each stroke revived my energy. I breathed in deeply and felt dizzy again. Colored lights with little circular dots swirled around me, beginning at my feet and spiraling upward until they reached my head.

I was now standing without knowing how I got to my feet. Tamrin was gone, but King Solomon and the archangels Metatron and Michael all smiled at me. Metatron's hands were extended, and he seemed to be motioning for the swirling lights and dots to circle around me. With each rotation, I felt more conscious of myself and my surroundings.

I saw a bench, and I guided myself to gently sit. "What happened?" I scratched my head.

Solomon sat beside me, putting his right hand behind my back in a supportive way. "The Ark's energy clashed with your own," he said. "You were upset about Hiram's death, and your explosive emotions almost triggered your *own* death."

Hiram! The night's memories were cloudy. "What happened to Hiram?" I breathed the question, not sure that I wanted to hear the answer.

Solomon answered, "Three of Hiram's assistants were jealous that they weren't being apprenticed into master masonry. They wanted Hiram's secrets, and when he wouldn't divulge them, the men took revenge by purposely botching the formula for the melted bronze. As Hiram went to pour the molten liquid into his mold, everything ignited. Hiram wanted to save his sculpture and got trapped in the flames. He died heroically, in service to Adonai's Temple. You can be proud of him."

Solomon squeezed my arm affectionately and looked at me sympathetically. I allowed him to hold me while I softly cried. The thought of Hiram suffering was unbearable. I wondered if I could have somehow prevented his death.

"Not even *we* could prevent his death," the archangels assured me. Michael stepped forward and explained that he couldn't violate Hiram's free will by saving him—he could only warn him. "Which I did many times," he added. "Hiram heard my warnings about his assistants' growing resentment, but he felt it was more important to guard his masonry secrets. He made the choice consciously."

This information was somewhat reassuring, but I still wondered whether Hiram had suffered.

"I was there at his passing," Michael spoke softly. "I personally escorted his soul away from his body before he could experience pain. His only suffering was in watching his sculptural masterpiece miss the mark of perfection he intended. That is why we helped him channel the moon's energy so that *The Molten Sea* could be completed with the lily ring around its rim."

Angels worked with the energy of the moon? "I thought that you only connected with your God, Adonai," I said.

"And what do you think the moon's energy is made of?" asked Archangel Metatron. "No matter what name you use to describe God or Adonai, you are still describing the same universal and omnipresent energy. So Adonai's energy is the moon's, and vice versa."

My head was spinning again. I'd always thought of the moon god Ta'lab as so powerful that nothing—not even Almaqah, the sun god—could control him. Now Metatron was suggesting that the entire platform of my religious beliefs might be wrong.

"Not wrong," Metatron said gently, "just limiting. The moon is a powerful force because it is an aspect of the One powerful force that permeates the Universe. Now, you can use any name that you like to describe the One force. Solomon's people choose the word *Adonai,* so that is the name I use in describing the force that is behind the moon, sun, and stars."

I sat down and held my head to stop the throbbing sensations. My whole world felt upside down!

"What do you suppose holds the sun, moon, and stars in the sky?" Metatron asked without the slightest hint of condescension.

"I've never thought about it. I suppose the same thing that keeps me alive or that helps me stand upright. I've always thought that Almaqah, the sun, was the Creator of life."

"The sun does support life, definitely." Metatron sat next to me and put his arm around my shoulder. I leaned into him, loving his gentle yet strong demeanor. Solomon, on my other side, squeezed my hand supportively. Metatron continued: "Beyond the sun there is so much more! The entire Universe is glued together with an invisible but palpable force that people call

Adonai, God, or Yahweh . . . the force that holds the sun, moon, and stars in the sky."

"Is Adonai a god or a goddess?" I wondered.

"Both!" Metatron chuckled. Then, in answer to my confused expression, he explained, "Every seeming opposite is part of the One force, Adonai: hot and cold, dark and light, male and female. When we distinguish male from female, we create a 'duality focus,' which gives rise to feeling separated from Adonai and each other.

"All human beings have both male and female energy within them. The male energy is used for strength and protection, while the female energy is more nurturing and artistic."

I thought of the times I'd been called into leadership and had definitely felt like a male warrior. Then there were other occasions when I felt more feminine, such as when I was curling up in my bedroom with my beloved cat, Abby, or that instance when I danced after the worship ceremony.

"You focus upon a deity as being either male or female, because you're acknowledging the deity's specialties. For instance, your Almaqah is viewed as male because the sun's radiant heat and golden rays are symbolic of male strength. Yet the truth is that the sun is also nurturing and life giving, which are female traits—so Almaqah, just like any other strong male, has feminine qualities. And the reverse is true for females, in that they have male characteristics. This is why we say that Adonai is both the Mother and the Father of the Universe."

Metatron's words seemed truthful to me even though I still didn't quite understand all of his philosophies. There was something inherently trustworthy in him. I could feel his goodness and purity, and I sensed that he wasn't trying to convert me or convince me of anything. He was simply sharing information with me, out of loving intentions.

My thoughts turned to Hiram, and I worried whether his soul was okay. I missed him so much! Even though ours had been a brief relationship, I'd cherished every moment of our togetherness. I tasted the hot saltiness of my tears as I tried to conceive of my life without Hiram. *Why him? He was such a good man!*

Metatron held me while I cried. When I opened my eyes, I was lying in bed, and Mother was caressing me. I blinked at her, wanting to ask her a thousand questions, but I was too weary to converse, so I slept instead. I vowed to discover the secret Hiram knew . . . the one that had ultimately cost him his life!

CHAPTER 16

I didn't want to get out of bed the next day. Sarahil brought breakfast to my room and washed my hair, just as she used to do back in Saba. While I didn't feel like talking or eating much, I welcomed her comforting presence. Mother was still with me, too.

My whole body ached from crying and the deep gaping hole of missing Hiram. How happy we'd been together! Our connection had been sheer magic. Despite our language differences, we'd communicated perfectly with each other.

I'd fantasized about Hiram and me marrying and having children. We'd all live in Saba, and finally my life would be fulfilling and meaningful. But that dream had died the night before, damn it!

I gritted my teeth and pounded the bed with my fists so hard that Sarahil backed out of the room,

murmuring an excuse about fetching something. I didn't care what she or anyone else thought, though. I had a right to be upset. Hiram was so talented and good-hearted that I couldn't just let his death go without at least trying to help. Sure, the guards had captured his three murderers, who would definitely be executed, but avenging his death wasn't the point. I needed to help Hiram's work—and therefore Hiram—to live on.

I needed to learn what he had been hiding so that I could put his knowledge to good use in completing the temple and whatever other purposes he'd had in mind. But how would I find out what it was?

Hiram's funeral was held the next day, as the custom of Jerusalem calls for immediate burial. No one could locate any family for him, and someone said that they believed he'd been orphaned as a young boy. How little I'd known about poor Hiram!

Since he had no apparent friends or family members, King Solomon himself offered to lead prayers during the funeral. Traditionally, the Jewish prayer of mourning, called the Kaddish, is read at the service. However, since Hiram wasn't Jewish, Solomon offered nondenominational prayers of his own making instead:

> We toss the coin, but it is Adonai who controls
> its decision. The name of Adonai is a strong tower;
> the righteous run into it and are safe. Every word of
> Adonai proves true; He is a shield to those who take
> refuge in Him.

Hiram's body lay in a closed wooden casket, following traditional customs, which say that the soul of
the body ascends as it decays. He would be buried in a
cemetery set aside for non-Jews. I said a silent prayer
that Athtar, the Venus god who protected the dead,
would look after Hiram. Aside from Solomon's passionate prayer, the funeral seemed solemn and plain
to me. Perhaps I was unfairly judging it against those
of Saba, which were more like tributary festivals.

Solomon continued his eulogy:

> Adonai will not allow the righteous soul to fam-
> ish. Blessings are on the head of the righteous, and
> the memory of the righteous is blessed. The path of
> the righteous is like the first gleam of dawn, shining
> ever brighter till the full light of day. The memory
> of the righteous is blessed. A good name is more
> desirable than great riches; to be esteemed is better
> than silver or gold. Prudence will watch over you,
> and understanding will guard you, dear Hiram!

Solomon's voice trembled, and he coughed as he
wiped his eyes. Could he be grieving the loss of Hiram?

I hadn't known the two were that well acquainted. I'd always assumed that Hiram was a mere employee to the king.

After the funeral, Solomon walked directly over to me and asked, "Will you accompany me to the park?" His eyes were reddened and moist, with dark circles beneath them. I sensed that Solomon needed a friend, someone with whom he could totally be himself. And I could definitely relate to the emptiness that accompanies a royal title—I was feeling it, too.

Solomon requested that his guards give us plenty of space, which they were reluctant to do, considering the previous night's murder. Still, they did stay far enough away that I felt I could talk openly with the king without fear of saying something that the populace's rumor mill would pounce upon. Members of royalty had to be so cautious about everything they said and did!

A beautiful rosebush caught my attention as a bee busily flew between the blush-pink buds. "They must have just bloomed," Solomon commented, seeing the direction of my gaze. "They weren't here on our last visit." He reached out to a rose that was just blooming, and I feared that the bee, which had just landed there, would sting him.

"Watch out," I cautioned.

The bee climbed out of the flower onto Solomon's outstretched hand. He brought it up to his nose and said, "Hello there, little fellow! Would you mind if I took this rose for my lady?" Solomon put his ear to the bee as if to listen for the answer. I worried that the insect would sting his face!

The king lowered his hand onto another rose, and the bee hopped off as if nothing had happened. Solomon gently snapped off the blossom that the bee had formerly inhabited and handed it to me. I inhaled its sweet perfume gratefully, happy to have a pleasurable moment to lighten my mood. I looked at the bloom and then at Solomon, whose eyes gazed at me with longing and loneliness. I wondered if I could do anything to ease both Solomon's heart and my own.

A riddle! "I can help you with that, honey!" Mother chimed into my right ear as Solomon and I continued walking along the park's garden path.

Mother! I snapped back, resenting her intrusion.

"I've created a list of riddles for just this occasion!" Mother said, unfurling a long scroll.

She started to read me the first one when I interrupted: *I can do this myself, Mother.* I was surprisingly calm as I explained, *I must do this for myself. I need to know that I can think of riddles and other ideas on my own.* Then I quickly added, *But I do appreciate your offer of help!*

"Well, I'm here if you need me, honey," Mother replied.

Actually, Mother, I'd prefer that you left us completely alone for this afternoon—no offense!

"Okay, honey. I won't peek in on you. But remember that I'm always within earshot. If you need me, just call." As she left, I felt an air-pressure change by my head. I looked at Solomon to see if he'd noticed anything, but he appeared lost in his own thoughts. Perhaps he, too, was talking with *his* angels!

I coughed, and Solomon looked at me. As he kissed my cheek and pointed to two swans swimming side by side in the pond, I forgot all about my idea to tell him a riddle. The swans stopped by the water's banks, and Solomon produced a handkerchief from his pants pocket. He ceremoniously opened the white cloth to reveal dried corn, which he poured into my hand, keeping a bit for himself.

Stuffing the cloth back into his pocket, Solomon urged me to extend my palm, fingers flat and together, to feed the swans. I watched one of the birds push his large dark bill against Solomon's hand. My shoulders tensed, as I feared he'd bite Solomon, but I needn't have worried, for the swan gently nibbled on the seed and not his flesh. The other one seemed to wait for me, so I nervously opened my palm, but then drew it back as the swan approached me.

"It's okay," Solomon reassured me, gently petting the swan's head. "She won't bite you, I promise." The king put his hand with mine, and we created a two-handed cup for both swans to feast together. I giggled as their bills tickled my palm. When they were finished eating, Solomon helped me pet the female swan, who seemed to enjoy the affection. As they waddled back into the water, the male swan honked, and I swore that it sounded as if he were thanking us.

The two swans intertwined their necks as they floated beneath the shady branches of a graceful willow tree. I felt Solomon's gaze upon my own neck, and I flushed at the realization that he was having romantic fantasies about me. The intertwined swans sailed along the currents, making romance seem so simple and natural. It *would* be so easy to get involved with Solomon. He was gorgeous, kindhearted, and well situated; and he wanted me. Yet my heart was numbed by Hiram's murder and absence. I sighed deeply.

A flash of purple caught my eye, and I was grateful for the distraction from my thoughts and feelings. As I walked toward the purple patch, I saw that it was a water-lily blossom stretching to catch the sunshine. I crouched to gaze at its beautiful petals, which were a shade of violet similar to the colors I'd seen in desert sunsets on our journey to Jerusalem.

"It closes up each night," Solomon said, interrupting my thoughts.

"Excuse me?" I said.

"The water lily closes as soon as the light fades," he explained. "Kind of like people. When someone forgets about the beautiful light that shines within them and everyone, they close down. And then you can't see the person's colors."

I wondered if Solomon was making a metaphor about *me*. If so, what point was he driving at?

"Well, some people don't have much light within them," I muttered, thinking about Hiram's murderers. "How could they be so cold and uncaring as to purposely kill Hiram? I fail to see any light radiating in *their* hearts!"

"Treasures of wickedness profit nothing, but righteousness delivers from death. Adonai won't allow good people to go hungry, but instead keeps evil people from getting what they want." Solomon smiled widely and hummed a tune as he wrote his words in a little notebook he kept in his pocket. He seemed very amused by his clever phrase.

Solomon's attitude stung. I walked down the sloping bank toward the pond. How could he be so cavalier and philosophical about Hiram's murder? Didn't he care whether Hiram had suffered . . . and how *I* was suffering without Hiram? Even the daisies enraged me as they tried to cheer me up with their sunshine-yellow smiles. I snapped three from their stems and threw them into the pond.

I continued stomping toward the swan couple, who I hoped somehow would give me some sympathy. After all, they knew what true love was.

"So do you, Makeda!" I heard Mother's voice again.

Mother! Things were now really going from bad to worse.

"I know I agreed to leave you alone, so I'll just stay for a moment to tell you one thing: Solomon is true, Makeda," Mother said rapidly, probably because she knew that my patience was wearing thin. "He loves you deeply with an open heart, without any hidden agendas. He and your future child are your destiny."

"But Mother, you know that I'm still in love with Hiram!" I snapped at her aloud, not caring what Solomon thought and ignoring her preposterous comment about a child.

"Just keep an open mind with him, Makeda. Although he's extremely powerful, he's also very sensitive. He's doing the best he can in trying to express his feelings to you," Mother said softly before vanishing.

Every time she appeared and disappeared, the air pressure pushed and suctioned around my head and shoulders, as if I were ascending and descending from very high mountain peaks. As I rubbed my forehead, I felt a warmth around my neck.

"Is everything okay?" Solomon said, his hand gently massaging my shoulder muscles. Despite my foul mood, I found myself relaxing into his strong, gentle touch. My body was betraying me by leaning into Solomon's massage!

"Hiram was an amazing man," he said, my shoulders stiffening at the sound of the architect's name. As I turned, Solomon's hands dropped to his sides. Sunlight filtered through willow-tree branches, and the moving shadows emphasized his powerful jaws, high cheekbones, strong nose, and ever-vigilant eyes. I swallowed hard as I felt a twinge in my heart. *No!* I told myself. *I cannot allow myself to feel anything toward Solomon!* I vowed to suppress my feelings.

Solomon's dancing eyes searched mine, and he took my hands and brought them to his lips. Then he gently wiped my tears with an embroidered handkerchief. His quiet intensity reverberated in my body. I could feel his restraint in holding himself back from speaking of the emotions we could both sense.

As my tears fell, Solomon held me tightly. He was silent except for an occasional soothing sound, and he rocked me in a most comforting way.

Could I share my feelings about Hiram? Was Solomon, the wise and powerful king, able to objectively hear me grieve and set aside his own emotions about me?

"I will listen," I heard him say. I looked up gratefully, ready to tell him about my short-lived but very deep bond of love with Hiram. But instead of facing the king, I found myself eye to eye with Michael the archangel. I looked around and squelched a yell when I noticed that he and I were hovering off the ground!

From our aerial perspective, I watched Solomon tenderly hold and rock me. Colorful flowers and birds surrounded us. The scene's sweetness tugged at my heart, and I felt my fondness for Solomon increase.

"Every moment around the world, there are thousands of examples of love," Michael said to me. "You are watching it in action right now, which is the most powerful demonstration of the Divine energies. The more you notice and practice love in action, the more you will enjoy the dynamic flow of your life.

"Just as there are many beautiful flowers, so are there infinite varieties of love. That which you shared with Hiram will always remain here"—Michael pointed to my head—"and here." He pointed to my heart.

The beauty of the scene below me and Michael's tender words overwhelmed my emotions, and I lost all control. Tears cascaded down as I yelled, "It's just not fair! Why didn't you protect Hiram? Why did he have to die!"

Michael held me above, while Solomon held me below.

When my tears had subsided, Michael placed his right palm just below my neck. His large hand covered my upper chest above my breasts. Heat radiated and tingled, and I wriggled uncomfortably as visions came into my mind's eye.

First, I saw my father on his deathbed, with me kneeling and crying, begging him to live. The sight of him shook me. I'd forgotten how much I missed him and how this ever-present pang of loneliness began the night that he died.

"Daddy!" I cried, trying to run into my vision. Instead, though, I saw myself nearly three years earlier as I desperately searched for ways to keep him alive. I had tried herbs, potions, spells, prayers, and incantations, but still my father had died.

"So, too, did your faith die that day," Michael said, patting my heart.

He was right. My naïve belief had been replaced with cynicism and distrust, and I only said my daily prayers out of habit and duty.

"Your distrust has also extended to relationships," Michael commented.

"Excuse me?"

"Your fear of being hurt has caused you to shun them," he said matter-of-factly.

Now I was angry. "That's not true! I had a great relationship with Hiram."

"Did you?" Michael asked. "It seems to me that you both spent time together but did not truly connect. There was the language barrier, for one. And second, it was a forbidden relationship, so the guilt factor hung over you during your very short time together."

"I loved him!" I snapped.

"You loved the idea of love without commitment, without real involvement, and without any emotional intimacy."

"Why are you being so mean to me?" I cried.

"I'm a truth-teller," Michael said. "Many dislike my bluntness, yet I always have solutions available for those who are ready."

"Solutions?"

"Yes, you and Hiram loved each other to the degree of your capacity to love. Your attraction toward each other was immediate and lasting because your hearts were attuned to the same frequencies based upon similar backgrounds and experiences. You see, Hiram was also grieving the loss of his family, and like you, he had shielded his heart from further pain by numbing his emotions."

"So we were attracted to each other because we felt safe? Because we wouldn't be hurt? What's wrong with that?" I felt tense, unsure of Michael's motives or what point he was trying to make.

"Your mutual attraction was based upon mutual woundedness," Michael said gently as I bristled with irritation. "It's possible that two emotionally wounded people can heal each other. However, there's an alternative solution."

There was that word again: *solution*. "Okay, I'm listening," I said, braced for what Michael would tell me.

"Any human can call upon the Divine for help in healing emotional wounds, to return the heart to its original pristine state. A healed heart is an open river through which maximum emotional energy runs, unfiltered and unfettered. A healed heart experiences the greatest heights of joy, bliss, and love. And most important, it welcomes love."

"Very poetic, yet completely impractical," I declared, with arms folded across my chest. "Everybody's heart is wounded in some way! We're talking Earth life here, not heaven!" *Now* who was being the truth-teller? I was proud of my assertiveness.

Michael seemed unfazed. Vivid and glowing purple light trailed out of his palms as his hands circled a few inches from my body until my legs and arms glowed like bright stars on a clear evening. Michael continued cocooning me in purple light, which felt so pleasant that I didn't think to stop him.

He then extended his hands like an artist painting a wall of purple light, which hovered in front of us. A bluish glow from its center began to move and take the form of a man.

"Father!" I gasped, watching a moving picture of my dad, Mother, and myself in earlier and happier times. The sight of him knocked the wind out of me. I tried to sit down, until I discovered that I couldn't reach the ground or any of the benches below me. I was weightless, and also helpless as I watched endless movies of my childhood. Ten minutes into them, I was a puddle of tears.

Michael held me, gently whispering words of comfort and encouragement. "Yes, that's it . . . allow your heart to open and heal. . . . It is safe to feel all of the colors, depth, and emotions of love . . . feel it all. . . ."

I surrendered the last shred of control over my emotions as I watched Father surprise me with a doll for my fifth birthday. How I loved that doll! How I loved my father!

"I miss him!" I cried as Michael held me. "Why does Mother visit, but I never see my father?"

"Because you have not forgiven him for leaving," Michael said after a long pause.

"You mean that he's mad at me? And he's avoiding me?" I broke down, sobbing at the thought.

Michael held me tightly. "Your father loves you, and he is not angry at all. In fact, he watches over you and is quite proud of you. It is not he who is avoiding you—it is the other way around."

"What do you mean?!" I screamed. "I would give anything to see Father again!" I tried to get away from Michael and rejoin Solomon in the park, but I remained stationary.

"I know you are upset," Michael said calmly. "But there is a solution. There is *always* a solution. Your anger about your father's passing has caused you to avoid thinking about him. You have stuffed down the emotions of grief as a way of coping with your loss. Yet your feelings are perfectly normal, and I can help you work with them.

"Everyone feels the same emotions when someone they love dies. Everyone experiences anger toward the person who died, toward the Universe for letting it happen, and toward themselves for not preventing the loss. Everyone feels shame, guilt, loneliness, regret, and other emotions . . . they are normal.

"But as long as you stuff down awareness of these emotions instead of allowing yourself to feel them, you create a wall between yourself and other people, living and deceased. Bottling up emotions closes the heart to love in all its many forms."

Michael's words rang true deep within, and I looked up to see Mother standing next to me, nodding with approval. "He's right, Makeda," she said sweetly. Yes, I had to admit, he *was* right. The truth was that I *had* pushed away my feelings following Father's death. It was all so overwhelming at the time, with my immediate coronation as queen and my new royal duties. I hadn't had time to deal with emotions—I had to be strong.

"There's strength in facing your feelings," Michael said. "Are you ready?"

I felt trepidation, as if a physician were downplaying how painful his procedure would be. Yet I truly did want to reunite with Father, and for that reason alone, I agreed to experience Michael's solution.

"What do I need to do?" I asked.

"Just be willing to forgive your father," Michael replied. "Your willingness is the magic key that allows the Divine light to illuminate the places within you that have been previously darkened by unforgiveness. Just breathe and be willing to release that unforgiveness in exchange for everything you desire."

I nodded and breathed deeply as Michael waved his hands over me, surrounding me with purple light. He whispered, "Imagine that your father is standing right in front of you. Keep an image of him in your mind's eye. Now, hold the intention of seeing the glow of Divine light within your father. You might see a whitish radiance within his stomach region."

At first, I couldn't see anything. I could feel a sense of my father, but I was unsure whether I was imagining this or not. With Michael's steady reassurance, I relaxed and stopped trying to make something happen; instead, I allowed the vision to come to me. I just breathed and thought of Father, and very soon I saw a picture of him in my mind. Then the image moved, and I saw scenes from my childhood.

Michael guided me to focus on my father's stomach area and imagine that I could see a glowing light inside of his body.

"I see it! I see it!" I grabbed Michael excitedly. "I see this glowing cloud of light inside my father. It's in his heart and chest area!"

"Perfect," said Michael. "Now ask this light to grow until it completely fills the inside of your father's body."

The instruction seemed odd, but I trusted Michael, so I breathed and willed my father's inner light to increase. Soon, his entire body glowed with a pulsating illumination. It kept growing until I could no longer see Father.

"Step into the light with him," Michael instructed.

Although I had no idea how to do this, I decided to try. I visualized myself stepping forward into the scene of glowing light. Sure enough, it worked! I dissolved into the ball of illumination until neither Father nor I were visible—there was just light.

My body shuddered and shook while Michael said, "Be willing to release any judgments; feelings of betrayal, fear, guilt, and shame; or any other toxic forms of unforgiveness."

Waves of energy reverberated and exited my body as Michael guided me to continue breathing deeply. "Be willing to release any old anger toward anyone, including yourself," he said. "Let it go . . . let it go . . ."

Memories of old pain flooded my mind. Long-forgotten instances of having my feelings hurt came to the surface and then were carried away on blankets of love. I saw Hiram, and felt my anger toward his murderers sweep away.

"You do not have to forgive the person's actions," Michael explained, "just the person, because holding grudges puts barriers between you and love. Keep going! You are doing a great job releasing the toxins from your body and mind."

I closed my eyes as my physical self felt blissfully light and tingly. My chest glowed warmly, and I felt happier than I had in ages, probably since I'd been a little girl.

When I opened my eyes, I was sitting on the grass next to Solomon. He leaned forward, and I surprised myself by allowing him to touch my face. He gently flicked a tear from my cheekbone and showed it to me. "What's this for?" he asked with such tenderness that I cried even more.

He held me while I lost control and sobbed helplessly into his strong shoulder. I felt him breathing and had the strange thought: *Oh, he's a real person!* I realized that I'd previously judged Solomon to distance myself from getting to know him.

The strength of my emotions surprised me, but I knew that Archangel Michael had helped awaken deep feelings within me. I wasn't sure that I liked them, although I sensed that the process was healthy for me. This must be what Mother called "opening your heart."

I wiped my eyes, worried that my kohl eyeliner must have dribbled down my face. Solomon handed me his handkerchief, and I wiped my face off. "You look beautiful, Makeda," he said with smiling eyes. He kept looking at me without talking, with an unspoken question about the source of my tears.

"I've just been thinking about my father," I said softly, almost inaudibly. I wasn't sure how much I wanted to reveal to Solomon. After all, I hadn't told anyone but Sarahil about my feelings regarding Father, and even she didn't know everything. Truly, I wasn't even aware of my feelings myself!

"I loved my father, too." Solomon sighed. Was that a tear falling from *his* eye? I reached out to wipe it away and connected with Solomon's eyes. I felt as if I were spinning, falling forward into them, losing awareness of myself and where I was.

Solomon's voice jolted me: "He was ill for quite some time, so I knew that his death was inevitable. Still, nothing prepared me for the shock of losing a parent: the silence after he was gone, the void where his voice and energy once roamed the palace, his advice and teasing, and even the things that once annoyed me about him. I still miss him. . . ."

"Me, too," I mused. "I mean—my father, not yours! Not that there's anything wrong with your father that I wouldn't miss him . . ." I was digging myself into a deeper trench with my awkward words, so I stopped speaking.

"I knew what you meant," the king said reassuringly. "When did your father die?"

The words made me wince. I paused. Did I really want to talk about this? "Over two years ago," I finally replied.

"So it's still fairly recent," Solomon said. "My father passed away several years ago. It was tough at first. My brother and some others were really upset and jealous that I'd been given the crown. My mother was beside herself with grief, even though she continued to be a wonderfully supportive parent to me. And I had huge shoes to fill, because *everyone* loved my father!"

"Yes, my father was deeply loved, too." I sighed, tears falling again. "The hardest part is when I want to share some exciting news with him or ask his advice. That's when I remember, *Oh, he's not here anymore.*"

Solomon put his arm around my shoulders, and we cried for our fathers together. My heart swelled with gratitude at the king's supportive friendship. As I kissed his cheek in gratitude, more tears welled up in his eyes. I gently wiped his cheeks as they flowed. Solomon held my hands next to his lips and looked at me deeply.

"There are three things too wonderful for me to understand," he said. "No, make that four! First, how an eagle glides through the sky." He kissed my hands and continued: "Second, how a serpent crawls upon a rock. Third, how a ship finds its way across the heaving ocean." Solomon sighed, wiped his eyes, and said, "And fourth, the growth of love between a man and a woman.

"I'm in love with you," he admitted, his eyes underscoring his words. "I'll do anything within my power to make you happy."

I didn't feel like talking, though. Instead, I leaned into Solomon while he held my shoulders. The sky glowed shades of pink and orange: time to return to the palace.

Solomon drove his chariot slowly, with one arm holding me tightly. I felt safe and very loved, but still fragile from the emotions and images I'd experienced. That night, I slept more deeply than I had in ages.

CHAPTER 17

I awoke with a start, wondering if I'd just been dreaming or if I'd really seen Father and Hiram. I sat up in bed, drinking water and reviewing the memories of the wild dream.

Father had appeared to me first, looking young, happy, and healthy. He reassured me that he loved me very much and that he was sorry his passing had caused me pain.

"It was my time to go," he explained, although I really didn't understand what that meant. Father showed me where he "lived": in a beautiful silken tent near a river and flower-field valley. He showed me how he watched over me and was always within earshot should I need his help or companionship. "You won't be bothering me at all if you call for me," he said.

Then Hiram appeared, and I hugged him like a dear old friend or even a brother. Both he and Father told me that my life purpose was important and that I needed to fulfill it.

They explained that Solomon truly loved me and it was important for me to be open to his affections. They said that I'd return to Saba soon, and that my visit to Jerusalem would forever change me and my commonwealth in a positive way—and that I'd inspire other women with my feminine strength.

I had no idea whether it was night or nearly daybreak, but I knew that I couldn't sleep any longer. I bundled my robe around my nightgown, slipped on some shoes, and walked outdoors. The guard was slumped over, sleeping outside the courtyard; and even the donkeys, horses, and camels near the stables were quiet.

I walked across the path toward the brush-filled desert sand, which glowed in the moonlight, stubbing my toe along the way. I yelped in pain and sat on a smooth boulder to rub my foot. My gaze wandered upward toward the shimmering sky. One very bright star glowed multiple colors, like a sparkling jewel.

"That's Sirius," said a voice above me. Startled, I looked up to see Solomon standing next to me, also wearing a robe. "I couldn't sleep either," he explained, sitting beside me on the boulder. I shivered in the nighttime coolness, and Solomon put his arm around me. I was grateful for his body heat and snuggled in closer. My toe was throbbing, and a wetness told me that it was bleeding. But I didn't want to call attention to my Jinn feet, so I didn't say anything.

I felt so comfortable in Solomon's arms, almost as if I'd known him for a long time. This was different from the fiery magnetism I'd experienced with Hiram. Solomon's arms were a solid foundation where I could grow roots and stay for a while. And I loved that he spoke my language so that we could actually communicate verbally!

Still, my heart grieved for Hiram, and I didn't think I was capable of having another passionate relationship so soon.

"We'll take it slow," Solomon whispered in my ear. Was he reading my thoughts? I looked above his shoulders to see if the archangels, or even my mother, were feeding him information. But for once it appeared that Solomon and I were truly alone.

I felt sleepy, yawning as I rested my head on Solomon's shoulder, the same one that I'd cried on the night before. Solomon's steady heart rate slowed my breathing, and I felt myself drift off. While the dawn sky came alive with birds and stars, my mind finally rested in a quiet state of sleep.

I don't know how long I slept, but I do remember the sound of music awakening me. The beautiful strains, like a choir of voices combined with exotic musical instruments, lured me from my slumber. I opened my eyes, expecting to see an orchestra or some musicians, but Solomon and I were the only people in sight.

"Are there birds nearby?" I asked, looking around.

Solomon kissed my head and said, "No, my love. You and I are delightfully alone. Why do you ask?"

I rubbed my eyes and explained how I'd heard the most wonderful sounds upon awakening.

"The music of the spheres," Solomon muttered.

"I've heard that phrase before," I replied, stretching my arms to lose the last bit of sleepiness, "but I don't remember where."

"From me!" a voice to my left announced. As my eyes adjusted, I saw the Archangel Metatron spinning a brightly colored geometric shape in between his hands. It emitted a buzzing and swirling sound, similar to the music I'd just heard.

"Metatron!" Solomon and I cried in unison.

The tall archangel looked at me and said, "All physical matter is composed of frequencies and vibrations that create sound, and you—like many people—are more open to hearing those sounds when your consciousness is relaxed. So the music of the spheres is audible during meditation and while awakening from a deep sleep. You heard the sound of creation, which is in perpetual motion."

Solomon smiled and stood up, reaching his hand out to mine. "Would you like to see a demonstration of what Metatron is talking about?"

I felt an air-pressure change around my head, and the familiar scents of Mother as well as Hiram drifted through the air. Then we were standing outside the temple, instantly transported without any ceremony or invocation.

"Thoughts create instant results." Metatron winked at me in answer to my silent question of how we'd arrived at the temple so rapidly. "You see, all words— whether spoken, written, sung, or thought—create reverberations like ocean waves. Allow me to demonstrate."

The spinning cube still in one hand, Metatron grabbed a tall drum from the ground with the other and sprinkled some fine desert sand across its top. Next, he poured a thick silver metallic liquid on top of a second drumhead. He and Solomon loudly chanted a word that sounded like *Yawd*. As their deep baritone voices merged, the sand and the silver liquid vibrated and formed a large circle on each drumhead.

Then they chanted other beautiful but unfamiliar words: *Yawd Hay Vawd Hay.* As their voices enunciated each vowel, the circle of sand and the silver liquid expanded into beautiful, symmetrical designs. Remarkably, the gleaming fluid seemed to defy gravity and didn't spill over the sides of the flat drumhead as long as the chanting continued.

There was something familiar about the design of the geometric forms on the drums, with their star patterns in the center. Then I realized they were the same shape that Metatron held in his hands.

"As I said to you before, everything in this world is constructed from one of five geometrical shapes, all of which are made from vibrational patterns." The cube that Metatron held disassembled itself into five shapes:

Tetrahedron

Cube

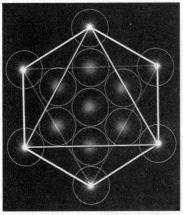

Octahedron

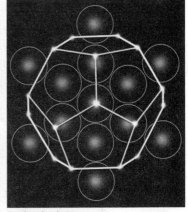

Dodecahedron

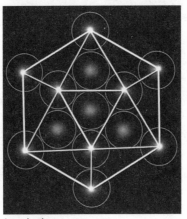

Icosahedron

Then the shapes re-formed together, suspended
between Metatron's outstretched hands. "These shapes

are all vibrations like words. That is why we call the all-encompassing worlds the *Universe,* which means 'one word.' This shape that you see me holding and which is displayed upon the drumheads is the culmination of all five geometrical forms. It's a visual representation of creation and the Universe.

"Let me show you this process in action," Metatron took my hand and cloaked Solomon and me in his wings. When he unfurled them, we were in a different location. "This is an outer wall of the temple, which is nearing completion."

I watched in wonder and awe as a group of people sat in a semicircle playing musical instruments in the most delicious harmony I'd ever heard. Singers of various vocal ranges chanted in unison with the notes. In front of these figures smooth, man-sized rocks levitated, just like my stone necklace had done (and was doing again!). Workers guided the floating rocks into place on the wall.

"Religious protocol says that temples and other sacred buildings cannot be constructed with metal tools, since weapons are made of metal. Anything that is used to kill a human being cannot be employed to build Adonai's Temple. Adonai gave specific instructions to David that no sound of a hammer or saw be emitted from the construction of his temple."

"So the entire temple was made from music?" I'd never heard of anything like this. "Tamrin told me that you worked with demons to construct it!"

Solomon laughed loudly and wiped his eyes. "You mean that old rumor's still circulating?" Then he calmly explained how the Hebrew words for *demons* and *musicians* were often confused. "Why would I employ demons—the Shaytan—to build Adonai's home? The word that Tamrin was thinking of was *shiddah* or *shiddot,* which is Hebrew for 'singers' or 'musicians.'"

I really needed to talk with Tamrin about brushing up on his Hebrew.

Metatron continued the discussion: "Many sacred buildings around the world were constructed in the same manner, such as the great pyramids of Egypt and the stone circles in Europe. The quartz crystal within granite rock readily entrains its vibrations to sound and music, so no matter how large or heavy it is, it can easily be transported and used to build with.

"When the sacred name of the Creator—*Yod He Vod He*—is chanted, the molecular structure of everything in creation is aligned in a process called 'entrainment,' as you saw in the dancing sand patterns upon the drumhead. The *Ah* sound in the Hebrew words *Yod* and *Vod* mirrors the original sound of creation. As I mentioned to you some time ago, all religions use the *Ah* sound in their name for the Creator, such as God, Adonai, Nada Brahma, Ra, Baal, and so forth.

"When the sacred *Ah* sound is chanted while accompanied by harmonic fifth octaves of music, waves of energy—similar to the ocean's mighty swells—can move objects of any size. This action is caused by the space between the twelve fifths of each octave, which holds them apart like a nautilus shell circling around itself with its lines never touching. The higher the pitch, the more intense the vibrations become, much like a soprano's voice shattering a crystal goblet.

Metatron pointed to a small pink Mediterranean gecko climbing straight up a wall. "See how this lizard sticks to vertical planes? He's using the same levitation principles as the rocks that float. The space and particles of energy in between the gecko's toes and that wall form a friction that causes gravity to reverse itself. There are male and female, positive and negative, energies colliding and connecting in that very small space between his toes and the wall."

"I used this method for building temples when I lived as a mortal man known as Enoch in an ancient land called Atlantis. There we understood the science of vibration and resonance so much that just by uttering a word such as *fire,* a flame would instantly begin burning from out of nowhere. When the misuse of this method led to Atlantis's demise, much of the knowledge fell into the ocean along with the land itself.

"Fortunately, I was intuitively forewarned about the coming flood, so I chiseled the information on stone pillars that I knew could survive the waters. I brought those pillars to this very Mount of Moriah and buried them. They sit today at the front of the temple as reminders that our knowledge must always be used in service of Adonai and never for personal gain.

"At the end of my mortal life, I was able to continue with my teaching work by transmuting into a higher-dimensional body known as the archangel who is standing before you today."

Then Metatron and Solomon began chanting the same words again: *Yawd Hay Vawd Hay.* The orchestra played in perfect harmonies with their chants, using different octaves of the same note. I looked down and noticed that my toe had completely healed. Even the dried blood was gone! My body buzzed with vibration, and my feet seemed light enough to levitate. Thoughts left my mind, and all I could see in my physical and mental sight was white light.

When I woke up, I was somehow tucked into my bed. Had the musical levitation been a dream? Or was it the information that was so valuable and secret that it had led to Hiram's death? My mind raced with unanswered questions, so I decided to go for another walk in the fresh early-morning air.

CHAPTER 18

As I climbed the stony pathway to the nearby hill, I wondered about the very foundation of my spiritual life. Lately, my sun-worship ceremonies had felt empty, as if I were just going through the motions. All of Solomon's talk, and now Metatron's demonstration, had caused me to question my fundamental belief that the sun was the supreme being.

I knew sunlight was necessary for life to exist, but what confused me was the question: *Did the sun actually create life, or did it just nurse it along after it already existed?*

I was happy to have the moon still overhead to accompany me along the trail, illuminating my steps with its lovely blue-white sheen. I sat on a smooth, large boulder and looked up at its crescent form. "Beloved moon god Ta'lab, please help me understand the concept of creation and the Creator!"

A beam of blue-white light surrounded me, glowing so brightly that it obliterated the scenery. I could only see its radiance. I felt the boulder and my body shake, as if the earth were quaking. A voice coming from both inside my head and the tunnel of blue-white light communicated to me: "All is vibration. You are vibration. The air that you breathe is vibration. This light is vibration.

"The first creation of vibrations is nonphysical forms of light, sound, and smell. When you focus upon these nonphysical vibrational forms, you elevate your consciousness to a higher dimension. That is why sound and light can move and affect denser physical forms of vibration such as human bodies and the stones in the temple.

"Vibrations can be slow or fast moving. The higher ones are lighter, so they're able to levitate and transcend the so-called laws that govern physical matter, which vibrates at much slower rates. Human emotions are like the spectrum of colors within rainbows of light. The hot and warm shades such as red and orange have the slowest and densest vibrations, just like the hot emotions of anger and jealousy; while the cooler colors have the highest, fastest, and lightest vibrations, just like the cool emotions of peacefulness and bliss.

"Try chanting the *Ah* sound," the voice suggested.

I looked around, a bit self-conscious about following this suggestion in case anyone in the palace might hear me. Not only would it be embarrassing to be discovered, but I also worried about releasing the dangerous secret that proved to be Hiram's demise.

The colors swirling around me turned from white-blue to a distasteful shade of yellow mixed with gray. I wondered if the fog had moved in around me, but the voice said, "The colors of your emotions are always visible to those who allow themselves to see and feel energies. You often block this ability in yourself because you don't want to acknowledge the effect that lower emotions, such as the worry and self-consciousness you just felt, have on you."

The voice asked me to breathe in and out deeply while imagining a happy memory. I was surprised when the first thing that popped into my mind was Solomon and me in the park, laughing and picking flowers. As I saw this romantic image in my mind, a beautiful blanket of clear purple, green, and blue light enveloped me.

"Now say *Ahhhhh*," the voice counseled gently. This time, instead of worrying, I followed its guidance and watched the colors around me swirl into ever-changing royal purples and bright blues mixed with silver and white sparkles. My heart swelled with warmth, and my shoulders and stomach relaxed more than they had in ages. I felt so giddy that I actually began to laugh!

My laughter echoed against the hillside and bounced back to me with a deep resonance, perhaps

an octave below the original sound. I looked down to see my dragon bloodstone necklace bouncing up and down gleefully at the high vibrations of my laughter and chanting.

"Congratulations," said the voice. "You've found the Creator."

CHAPTER 19

I had to find Solomon. It was now well into the morning, so I assumed that he must be in his office chambers, as he normally was every day around this time. His guards waved me past, accustomed to my presence in the palace. Solomon's cup of tea was next to his desk chair, but he was gone.

"Michael! Metatron! Mother!" I called. "Where's Solomon?"

Michael was the first to appear. "Follow me," he said, beckoning me.

We walked down a large corridor that ended with a doorway leading to a narrow outdoor path. From the looks of it, the pathway didn't appear to be used that much, as long weeds were growing in between the stones. We descended a very uneven stone staircase until we reached a large building that I hadn't remembered seeing previously.

Michael put his hands to my lips, indicating that I should remain quiet as he pushed open the doors. The thunderous noise of men arguing greeted our entrance. Solomon, seated on a very high platform behind a large wooden desk, was listening to them intently. Michael and Metatron stood on either side of him, whispering in his ear.

I turned to see how Michael had left my side so quickly and was shocked to find that he was still with me. I did a double take to verify that the figure I'd seen with Solomon was indeed him. Michael grinned widely and communicated wordlessly to me that he was unlimited in his ability to help many people simultaneously. For some reason, I found this "Mr. Perfect Archangel" ability annoying, until Michael communicated to me that I—and everyone—was unlimited, too.

"You only experience limitations because you believe that you are limited," he explained cryptically.

I decided that I'd think about Michael's profound words later. Right now I wanted to focus on Solomon's amazing power, light, and masculine energy as he decided which farmer among those present rightfully owned a disputed pasture. The king had never looked as handsome as he did right then. I wished I could have kissed him at that very moment.

Solomon hit his gavel hammer loudly on his desk, signaling that his decree—that the farmers should jointly share the work and the crops of the pasture—was final. The farmers left the courtroom smiling, and I was proud of Solomon for settling their dispute so wisely.

"He does this every day," Michael communicated, "often without needing our input at all."

My heart raced as my attraction grew for this amazing king. I wondered if my hesitation about his marriage proposal had put him off. I didn't want to lose him!

Solomon noticed my presence in the back of the courtroom, and his eyes and smile melted any insecurities I had about his affections. *He still loved me!*

He walked toward me, looking very stately and tall in his courtroom robes. "Makeda!" he purred. "I was just thinking about you!" Solomon escorted me past the court officers, who began talking among themselves. I realized that I was the only woman in the building. I certainly didn't intend to create a scandal for Solomon!

"Don't worry about idle gossips, who just spread strife. Whoever guards his mouth and tongue keeps his soul from troubles," Solomon reassured me as he opened the door to a private garden patio with high walls behind the courtroom building. "I was just about to have lunch. Please join me."

I looked at the sun and knew that it was nearly time for worship services, yet I really wanted to be with Solomon and tell him about my newly stirring feelings.

Forgive me, Almaqah and Tamrin, I thought as I said to Solomon, "Yes, I'd be happy to have lunch with you!"

As we shared a simple meal and juice, I listened to Solomon discuss the court cases he'd heard that morning. Some of them seemed so ridiculous in their basis that I laughed at the king's descriptions, yet he always showed compassion for those involved, no matter how far-fetched the claimant's case.

"Your own soul is nourished when you are kind. Whoever is kind honors Adonai," the king explained.

"You're a very kind and amazing man, Solomon," I said, my voice shaking.

Solomon guessed the source of my nervousness, and in a true show of compassion, he held my hands tightly so that I wouldn't need to voice the words myself.

"Makeda," he said, kissing my hands and holding them to his heart, "do you feel this beating within my chest? My heart beats for you alone. Please say that you'll marry me so that it can beat like this for all of my days."

My mouth felt dry. "Yes," I whispered, my voice barely audible.

Solomon's mouth opened, and he turned his head to one side. "Did you just say 'yes'?" he breathed the question.

"Yes!" I said brightly. "Yes, I *will* marry you. I will be your wife!"

Solomon picked me up with such speed and strength that I thought my joy was levitating and twirling me above the ground. We kissed as he held me in his arms. The sun was fully above us, and I could hear the strains of our afternoon ceremony's music from the palace courtyard.

"There will be a wedding!" Solomon announced as he carried me into the courtroom.

The men applauded and cheered enthusiastically: "Long live King Solomon and the Queen of Sheba!" Everyone's minds and hearts seemed wiped clean of malicious gossip in light of our happy news. Everything felt so right.

I discovered that the walking path between the courthouse and palace buildings was unused because Solomon rode his horse-drawn chariot for the short distance. The king adored riding in chariots, much as young boys enthusiastically rode on small wooden wagons.

Solomon waved ceremoniously with one hand and held me tightly with the other. I wondered if our entire married life would be on public display, but realized that Solomon's zeal couldn't be contained. I remembered the lesson I'd learned the night before about higher-vibrating emotions creating clear and bright colors, so I decided to relax and allow my enthusiasm to shine for Solomon and the crowd who waved to us as we neared the palace.

I could hear utensils scraping plates and chattering diners down the hallway as I stepped into the palace while Solomon gallantly held open the door for me. A large man exiting at exactly the same time ran right into me, and it wasn't until I'd disentangled myself from his large frame that I realized who he was.

"Tamrin!" I gasped.

"My queen," he whispered urgently, "I must speak with you." He turned toward Solomon and added, "Alone." Tamrin's face was red and his stature stiff as he abruptly hurried off toward where Sarahil waited.

I pretended not to notice Tamrin's upset demeanor and returned my attention to the more pleasant task of accompanying Solomon to his private chambers so that we could begin making our wedding plans. We walked by Tamrin and Sarahil, who both urgently motioned for me to step over toward them.

"Darling, could you please excuse me for a moment?" I said to Solomon, kissing his cheekbone, which was so exquisitely well defined. He seemed more handsome than ever. "Tamrin and Sarahil have probably heard about the wedding already. I'll meet you in your office chambers."

Tamrin and Sarahil grabbed my arms and took me to a private alcove in the hallway. In a heated voice

Tamrin demanded to know why I wasn't at the worship ceremony that day. "We were worried, Queen Balkis!" he whispered sharply. "You are our queen, and you're acting like a schoolgirl missing classes to be with her boyfriend!"

I looked at Tamrin. Was he jealous? Did he feel as if he were losing someone who was like a niece to him? I gave him and Sarahil a hug and told them about the wedding.

Tamrin swung me around sharply and looked at me so intensely that I squirmed as if my own father were about to pronounce a guilty verdict upon me. I swallowed hard as Tamrin said, "But you know the laws of Sheba won't allow you to marry, my queen! You are already and forever married to our sun god, Almaqah, whom you showed great disrespect to today."

How could I tell Tamrin that I'd decided to convert to Judaism and worship the Creator as Solomon did— that somehow I'd still acknowledge the sun, moon, and stars without deifying them? His eyes told me that I couldn't admit this information to him. Not yet.

"There's more, my queen," said Tamrin, leading me to a bench and motioning for me to sit. I gulped. "We've just learned about severe unrest in Saba. The people are unsure if you're ever returning, as they've heard rumors that you're moving permanently to Jerusalem. There's talk of a takeover of the commonwealth! My trade routes need attention, and the bottom line is that we must all return to Saba at once."

My head spun with this information. I hadn't realized that so many decisions were involved in my marriage, such as *Where would I live?* I could abandon my sun-god husband but not the people of Saba.

"When do we need to leave, Tamrin?" I asked, afraid to hear the answer.

"First thing tomorrow."

CHAPTER 20

"Makeda, my love, what's wrong?" Solomon was holding me as I caught my breath after running to his chambers following my conversation with Tamrin.

I couldn't talk, I was sobbing so hard. I loved Solomon and wanted to be in his arms forever. And I could fulfill that desire if I chose to abandon my commonwealth and all of its people to some egomaniacal despot who would take advantage of my absence. I just couldn't do that to the good citizens of Saba. My father and I had worked too long and hard to create a prosperous and peaceful land where everyone's needs were met and we were all happy and safe.

Fortunately, the archangels were with Solomon and me to ease the pain as we realized the necessity of parting ways. Solomon and I were soul mates in every way: being born into royalty, inheriting the crown after our fathers' passing, feeling passionate about spirituality and peacefulness, and fulfilling our life's purpose and destiny . . . no matter what.

So although the situation obviously angered and distressed him greatly, Solomon was able to be philosophical about it. His lifetime of dealing with difficult situations really showed through.

"We'll get married today then!" Solomon stood up and announced as if there were an audience, even though I was the only other person in the room.

He held my hand so that I'd stand next to him. "Let's do it now," he exclaimed, hurriedly pulling me out of his office and down the hallway.

"Where are we going?" I asked.

"To the temple!" he said as we both jumped into his finest chariot. "We're getting married!" he proclaimed several times along the way, to the delight of passersby.

I was glad that I'd worn one of my newer gowns that day with a romantic sweetheart neckline that highlighted the dragon bloodstone pendant my father had given to me—the thought of it stopped me.

"Father!" I began crying. "How I wish you could be with me right now at my wedding to give me away. Mother, I wish you were here, too."

I smelled a familiar scent and saw that Father; Mother; Hiram; and my sweet kitty, Abby, were with me. Tears filled my eyes upon sensing their presence and at the realization that my beloved cat had passed away in my absence. I missed Father, Abby, and my home in Saba so much! Well, at least they were with me now from their heavenly vantage point.

Solomon held me tightly as I wiped my tears with the inside of my bell sleeves. I wondered what I looked like right at that moment. I was grateful that Solomon made me feel beautiful even when I felt like an emotional mess.

The chariot stopped quickly and we jumped out and ran up the steps to the temple courtyard. Solomon called for the high priest. Someone found him and we stood between the two pillars while the startled priest said some impromptu prayers and asked us to sign a *ketubah*—marriage contract—which promised that Solomon would cherish, honor, support, and maintain me faithfully.

The high priest then pronounced us husband and wife. Solomon removed the golden ring from his finger and slipped it onto mine. As if by magic, it fit my left ring finger perfectly. I heard a screeching sound and looked up as the hoopoe bird circled above us. I swore that he was smiling.

Solomon held his body close to mine and said, "My love, my bride, I'll never give you up. Our souls will always be together, and I'll cherish you forever and ever." Then he closed his eyes, smiled widely, and kissed me with combined gentleness and passion.

How I wished that Solomon would rescue me from my dilemma of needing to return to Saba. If only the archangels could use their magic on time, slowing down the moments so that I could live with Solomon forever in that one remaining day.

Servants brought delicious spicy food into Solomon's bedroom foyer, where we sat at a beautiful carved table on upholstered lounge chairs, which had us reclining while eating. Solomon giggled as I fed him a spoonful of rice with vegetables and beans and some of the sauce dribbled down his chin. I kissed his chin and wiped away the sauce.

Finally, the servants left and we were alone in Solomon's bedroom chamber. The door echoed with a dull thud as the final attendant exited, and my heart suddenly had a mind of its own as I realized the extent of my wedding-night nervousness. Suddenly, I wanted to bathe.

As usual, Solomon was gracious, caring . . . and apparently psychic, because he offered to fill his large bathtub with flowers and oils for me to have a soak. I gratefully accepted, wondering if I should disrobe in front of him or demurely wait until after the tub was filled. Well, the decision was made as Solomon held out a freshly heated Turkish terry-cloth robe for me. I slipped out of my gown behind the robe, just inches from Solomon's breath. He couldn't see me, but we could both feel each other's excited presence.

As the king left the bathing room, I slipped into the deliciously warm water. The fragrance of the jasmine petals floating on the water's surface mingled with the floral oils of Solomon's alchemy. I closed my eyes and exhaled deeply, finally relaxing after the day's rapid pace and heady events.

"Is everything fine in there, my love?" Solomon called from the other room.

"Mmm," I purred in reply.

The lights dimmed so that all I could see was one candle, which appeared to float across the room until I realized that Solomon was holding it. He set it down on the basin and held out the robe to screen me as I dried myself on one of his thick and luxuriously soft towels.

When the robe was cinched around my waist, Solomon grasped my hand as if to show me a surprise. The bedroom glowed with dozens of red and white candles that flickered like starlight. He held out a beautiful carved box and said, "For you, my beautiful bride."

I opened its lid and gasped at the gorgeous gold-filigree tiara inside. I held it up and the candlelight sparkled across its diamonds, rubies, emeralds, and sapphires. "This is your crown as queen of my heart," he said with great emotion. I looked in the mirror and noticed that my face was glowing and flushed in a way I hadn't seen since my youth.

"You look incredible," Solomon observed as he sat on the edge of his large tufted bed. It had even more pillows than my bed back home in Saba, if that were possible!

Bless Solomon for being so gentle with me! He wasn't insistent and didn't manipulate me into his bed, but instead gave me the option of spending the night in an adjoining private guest room. As much as I wanted to consummate our marriage, everything had happened so quickly that I didn't feel that I was even *in* my body! My mind seemed to float somewhere in space, as if this were a pleasant, but still unreal, dream. Besides, both of our hearts were heavy with grief at the realization that we'd part ways in the morning.

Solomon tucked me into the softest bed I'd ever lain upon, and I immediately fell asleep despite my efforts to enjoy this last evening in Jerusalem with my new husband. How cruel and ironic that I'd had all of this time with Solomon and only now fully appreciated how much I loved him!

I woke in the quiet stillness of the night with a raging thirst. The salty, spicy meal that Solomon and I shared had parched my throat! I searched in the dark until I found the nightstand's water pitcher, but it was dry. Solomon's servants hadn't expected company, so they hadn't thought to fill it.

I stumbled in the dark and unfamiliar room, like a person in the desert, desperately seeking water. I held my hands in front of me, touching walls and walking gingerly to find my way. The loud clunking noise of a brass container falling on the tile floor roused Solomon from his sleep, and he moaned, "Yes, what is it?"

The sound of his voice stirred my heart, but my thirst was my more pressing concern. "I'm sorry, darling. I'm just looking for some water."

Solomon sat up and lit a candle to help me find him. He needn't have done so, as I could feel his larger-than-life presence.

"Here you go, sweetheart," he said, holding a large goblet filled with water to my lips. I sat down on the edge of his bed and soothed my mouth and throat with the satisfying liquid. "Would you like more?" Solomon offered, lifting up a full pitcher of water.

I gratefully nodded and held up my goblet for a refill. "The meal was spicy," Solomon remarked. "I've been thirsty tonight, too." He looked at me soulfully, and I knew that we shared the same wish that I didn't have to leave for Saba in the morning. Yet Solomon's royal upbringing gave him respect for the duty that spurred my departure.

A tear trickled down the left cheekbone of that gorgeous face, which inspired a kingdom to appreciate the Creator's wonders and delights. I kissed the tear, his cheek, and then his eyes. Solomon smiled, but I could feel his heart, which was heavy with loneliness. Finally, we'd found one another, as if in a dream from which we'd both soon awaken.

I don't know which one of us lay down on his bed first that night. All I remember is how wonderful his warm skin felt against my body. We didn't sleep the rest of the night. We couldn't.

The sounds of men and animals going about their morning activities was our unhappy announcement of the dawn's arrival. Solomon and I both sobbed as we lay in each other's arms, our hearts racked with the unfairness of having to put duty before personal pleasures. We could have easily stayed locked away in his bedroom for weeks had it not been for my promise to Tamrin that I'd be ready to leave right after breakfast. Thankfully, I could eat my last meal with Solomon in his chambers.

Like a woman with a death sentence hanging over her head, I savored some of my favorite foods as if they were my last bites in this lifetime. They might have been, as I didn't know how I'd ever live again without the companionship of Solomon by my side. Yet we were both duty bound to our thrones and our life purpose of steering our lands through eras of peacefulness and prosperity.

Sarahil brought my traveling gown to Solomon's bedroom so that I could spend every last minute with him. I walked in a daze to the awaiting caravan, where Tamrin was barking orders to men strapping supplies on the backs of our camels and donkeys. Somehow we were returning with even more material possessions than we'd brought to Jerusalem . . . yet, I was leaving my heart behind.

As we stood together one last time, I considered telling Solomon about my feelings. But he put his index finger to my lip as if to say, *There's no need to speak. I know. I feel it, too.* I was relieved that he understood. There were no words that could express the way in which my heart sang with joy for having loved him . . . or my overwhelming grief at having to leave him.

Tamrin called for me to get into my palanquin while Sarahil nervously paced between me and the caravan.

I twirled my wedding ring and stared at its six-pointed star and inset crystals. Solomon held it to my heart, and we both exhaled loudly.

"You'll both be forever connected throughout time," a voice said. We looked up to see the archangels Michael and Metatron hovering between us, pointing to a tunnel of swirling pink, green, and purple light. It was like a bridge that joined my body and Solomon's, a connection of light linking our hearts. "You'll always love each other and feel each other's love through this conduit," the archangels explained.

As our caravan set off toward Sheba, I pulled back my palanquin's curtains and peered outside. Solomon was walking beside me. I held out my hand, and he continued to walk alongside, clasping it, until we reached far beyond the palace citadel. His guards hovered around him as the great king slumped over, racked with sobs. I too began crying at the thought that my actions had caused him such sorrow.

The palanquin filled with light, and my stomach fluttered with a quickening movement. Instinctively, I put my hand protectively over my abdomen.

My heart was filled with hope. New life was on its way, I just knew it.

AFTERWORD

Many people and legends claim to know what happened to Solomon and me after I left Jerusalem. Even our son, Menelik, has his version of the end of our tale. But only Solomon and I know the real story, so I've decided to set the record straight:

My pregnancy left me feeling tired, and I had enormous responsibilities to attend to when I returned to Saba. So, for the first few weeks, I only met with Solomon during my dreams.

I was surprised that what I missed most were our walks and discussions in the park. I found myself becoming increasingly despondent, which Sarahil said wasn't good for the baby growing inside of me. So although I hadn't used my Jinn magic for months, I decided that I *had* to visit my husband before I went insane from grief.

At noon on the day following this decision (there was no time conflict, since I'd stopped attending the solar-worship ceremonies after converting to Judaism), I stood on a smooth, flat stone; cupped my hands; and made a Statement of Empowerment. I closed my eyes, my heart fluttering with anticipation at surprising Solomon. But when I opened my eyes, I was still standing on the flat stone in Saba!

Frustrated and in tears, I tried again and again until the sun went down, and then when the moon rose, I tried once more . . . but nothing happened! I was exhausted when I crawled into bed. Thankfully, Solomon held me all through the night during our dream rendezvous.

The next morning, I was startled to see Mother sleeping beside me. My pillows were covered with smeared kohl, and the sheets were twisted around my legs. I wondered worriedly whether Solomon had lost interest in me and had somehow blocked my Jinn magic. Perhaps it wasn't safe for me to teleport with the baby inside my womb.

"Are you done?" Mother asked with a sleepy voice.

"Mother, why can't I transport myself to see Solomon?" I anxiously demanded to know, ignoring her sarcastic question.

Mother stretched her arms and yawned. "Don't you remember the night that Hiram was killed?" she nonchalantly answered.

My heart leapt at the horrible memory. Why was Mother being so irritating today? Didn't she realize how sensitive I was, with my pregnancy and growing grief over missing Solomon? "Of course I remember!" I snapped even more rudely than I'd intended, which made me realize the depth of my anger.

Mother continued: "Well, the night of Hiram's death, you were unable to teleport yourself to the temple because you were upset. In fact, you were almost killed because your grief clashed with the pure energy of the Ark of the Covenant."

"Yes, that's true, but what . . . ?" I was about to ask for a further explanation, but then I realized Mother's point. Jinn magic only worked when I was aligned with the sun, moon, and other physical energies. I'd forgotten Mother's earlier lessons, which had stated that the earth's natural state is joyfulness. "If you're not joyful, your energy won't harmonize with the sun's rays," she'd told me repeatedly.

"Okay, Mother, thanks!" I said. I was about to apologize for my earlier rudeness, but Mother put her fingers on my chin and lifted my eyes to meet hers.

"I love you, sweetheart," she said, softly kissing my nose. My heart swelled with warmth, and I felt hope that I'd be able to reach Solomon by focusing on my happiness being with Mother and my ever-growing baby.

So that was the first day I was able to send myself to Jerusalem. When I found Solomon, he was despondent as well. But then he saw my expanding belly and fell to his knees crying as he cradled my stomach. He kissed me until it was time for me to return to Saba—after all, we both had extensive royal duties to perform.

I visited Solomon frequently after that. People in the temple often didn't recognize me, as I changed in appearance through the years. Rumors started spreading of Solomon's many wives, which were all really me at various stages of my life.

In between my visits with Solomon, the hoopoe bird brought me beautiful love poems that the king handwrote in my Sabaean language.

But in the end, I don't think Solomon's sensitive heart could take my frequent absences, as he fell ill and never recovered. Of course I was there with him at the end. How could I not be? After all, we were soul mates, destined to spend eternity together; and as I write this to you from heaven, I assure you that Solomon and I are happily together . . . forever.

BIBLIOGRAPHY

Aithie, C. & P., *Yemen: Jewel of Arabia,* 2001. London: Stacey International.

Ashton, A., *Harmonograph: A Visual Guide to the Mathematics of Music,* 2003. Wales: Wooden Books, Ltd.

Bialik, H. N., and Y. H. Ravnitzky, eds., *The Book of Legends (Sefer ha-aggadah): Legends from the Talmud and Midrash,* 1992. New York: Schocken Books, Inc.

Biella, J. C., *Dictionary of Old South Arabic Sabaean Dialect,* 2004. Winona Lake, IN: Eisenbrauns.

Brooks, M. F., *Negus: Majestic Tradition of Ethiopia,* 2002. Kingston, Jamaica: LMH Publishing, Ltd.

Brown, R. K., *The Book of Enoch, Second Edition,* 2000. San Antonio, TX: GBTS Press.

Carillet, J.-B., G. Anderson, and P. Harrison, *Diving & Snorkeling Red Sea,* 2001. Victoria, Australia: Lonely Planet Publications.

Clapp, N., *Sheba: Through the Desert in Search of the Legendary Queen,* 2001. New York: Houghton Mifflin Company.

Collins, A., *From the Ashes of Angels: The Forbidden Legacy of a Fallen Race,* 2001. Rochester, VT: Bear & Company.

Farrar, F. W., *Solomon: His Life and Times,* 2005. Boston: Elibron Classics.

Ginzberg, L., *Legends of the Jews, Volumes 1 and 2,* 2003. Philadelphia: The Jewish Publication Society.

Hall, M. P., *The Secret Teachings of All Ages: An Encyclopedic Outline of Masonic, Hermetic, Qabbalistic and Rosicrucian Symbolical Philosophy,* 1988. Los Angeles: The Philosophical Research Society, Inc.

Hamblin, W. J., and D. R. Seely, *Solomon's Temple: Myth and History,* 2007. London: Thames & Hudson, Ltd.

Hancock, G., and R. G. Bauval, *Talisman: Sacred Cities, Secret Faith,* 2005. London: Penguin Books, Ltd.

Hancock, G., *The Sign and the Seal,* 1992. New York: Crown Publishers, Inc.

Holy Bible: New Living Translation, Second Edition, 2004. Carol Stream, IL: Tyndale House Publishers, Inc.

Hopkowitz, Y. Y., *The Wisdom of King Shlomo: A Collection of Medrashim and Aggodot from Our Sages about King Shlomo,* 1985. Jerusalem: Hopkowitz Publishing.

Huntley, H. E., *The Divine Proportion: A Study in Mathematical Beauty,* 1970. New York: Dover Publications, Inc.

Jenny, H., *Cymatics: A Study of Wave Phenomena and Vibration,* 2001. Newmarket, NH: MACROmedia Publishing.

Jones, C. L., *The Complete Guide to the Book of Proverbs: King Solomon Reveals the Secrets to Long Life, Riches, and Honor,* 2000. Union Lake, MI: Quinten Publishing.

Josephus, F., *Antiquities of the Jews, Volumes 1 and 2,* 2006. West Valley City, UT: Waking Lion Press.

Khan, H. I., *The Mysticism of Sound and Music: The Sufi Teaching of Hazrat Inayat Khan,* 1996. Boston: Shambhala Publications, Inc.

Knight, C., and R. Lomas, *The Hiram Key: Pharoahs, Freemasons and the Discovery of the Secret Scrolls of Jesus,* 2001. Gloucester, MA: Fair Winds Press.

Korotayev, A., *Ancient Yemen: Some General Trends of Evolution of the Sabaic Language and Sabaean Culture,* 1995. New York: Oxford University Press, Inc.

Lawton, J., *Silk, Scents & Spice,* 2004. Paris: United Nations Educational, Scientific and Cultural Organization.

Leeman, B., *Queen of Sheba and Biblical Scholarship,* 2006. Queensland, Australia: Queensland Academic Press.

Maier, P. L., ed., *Josephus: The Essential Writings,* 1988. Grand Rapids, MI: Kregel Publications.

Mardrus, J. C., and E. P. Mathers, trans., *The Queen of Sheba,* 1924. London: The Casanova Society.

Mitchell, T. J., *Rosslyn Chapel: The Music of the Cubes,* 2006. Northallerton, UK: Divine Art, Ltd.

Patai, R., *The Hebrew Goddess, Third Edition,* 1990. Detroit: Wayne State University Press.

Pearn, N. S., and V. Barlow, *Quest for Sheba: In the Footsteps of the Arabian Queen,* 2003. London: Kegan Paul.

Phillipson, D. W., *Ancient Ethiopia,* 1998. London: The British Museum Press.

Rappoport, A. S., *Myth and Legend of Ancient Israel, Volume 3,* originally published 1928, reprinted 2005. Whitefish, MT: Kessinger Publishing.

Razwy, S. A. A., ed., and A. B. Ali, trans., *The Qur'an: Translation,* 1999. New York: Tahrike Tarsile Qur'an.

Schippmann, K., *Ancient South Arabia: From the Queen of Sheba to the Advent of Islam,* 2001. Princeton, NJ: Markus Wiener Publishers.

Schneider, M. S., *A Beginner's Guide to Constructing the Universe: The Mathematical Archetypes of Nature, Art, and Science,* 1994. New York: HarperCollins Publishers, Inc.

Simpson, S. J., *Queen of Sheba: Legend and Reality,* 2004. Santa Ana, CA: The Bowers Museum of Cultural Art.

———, *Queen of Sheba: Treasures from Ancient Yemen,* 2002. London: The British Museum Press.

Tanakh: The Holy Scriptures, 1985. Philadelphia: The Jewish Publication Society.

Wallis Budge, E. A., trans., *The Kebra Nagast (The Glory of Kings),* 2007. Rockville, MD: Silk Pagoda.

Whiston, W., trans., and P. L. Maier, *The New Complete Works of Josephus,* 1999. Grand Rapids, MI: Kregel Publications.

👑 👑 👑

ABOUT THE AUTHOR

Doreen Virtue is a doctor of psychology with a passionate interest in studying the history of world religions and spirituality. She previously wrote about King Solomon in her book *Archangels & Ascended Masters* and in the *Ascended Masters Oracle Cards*. Doreen is the author of numerous popular books and other products, including the internationally best-selling *Healing with the Angels* book and card deck. She's been featured on *Oprah*, CNN, and *Good Morning America*, and in newspapers and magazines worldwide.

Doreen teaches classes related to her books and hosts a weekly call-in radio show on **HayHouseRadio. com®**. For information on her products, workshops, or radio show, or to receive her free monthly e-newsletter, please visit: **www.AngelTherapy.com**.

We hope you enjoyed this Hay House book. If you'd like to receive a free catalog featuring additional Hay House books and products, or if you'd like information about the Hay Foundation, please contact:

Hay House, Inc.
P.O. Box 5100
Carlsbad, CA 92018-5100

(760) 431-7695 or **(800) 654-5126**
(760) 431-6948 (fax) or **(800) 650-5115 (fax)**
www.hayhouse.com® • **www.hayfoundation.org**

Published and distributed in Australia by: Hay House Australia Pty. Ltd., 18/36 Ralph St., Alexandria NSW 2015 • *Phone:* 612-9669-4299 *Fax:* 612-9669-4144 • www.hayhouse.com.au

Published and distributed in the United Kingdom by: Hay House UK, Ltd., 292B Kensal Rd., London W10 5BE • *Phone:* 44-20-8962-1230 *Fax:* 44-20-8962-1239 • www.hayhouse.co.uk

Published and distributed in the Republic of South Africa by: Hay House SA (Pty), Ltd., P.O. Box 990, Witkoppen 2068 *Phone/Fax:* 27-11-467-8904 • orders@psdprom.co.za • www.hayhouse.co.za

Published in India by: Hay House Publishers India, Muskaan Complex, Plot No. 3, B-2, Vasant Kunj, New Delhi 110 070 • *Phone:* 91-11-4176-1620 *Fax:* 91-11-4176-1630 • www.hayhouse.co.in

Distributed in Canada by: Raincoast, 9050 Shaughnessy St., Vancouver, B.C. V6P 6E5 • *Phone:* (604) 323-7100 *Fax:* (604) 323-2600 • www.raincoast.com

Tune in to **HayHouseRadio.com®** for the best in inspirational talk radio featuring top Hay House authors! And, sign up via the Hay House USA Website to receive the Hay House online newsletter and stay informed about what's going on with your favorite authors. You'll receive bimonthly announcements about Discounts and Offers, Special Events, Product Highlights, Free Excerpts, Giveaways, and more! **www.hayhouse.com®**

If you'd like to receive a catalog of Hay House books and products, or a free copy of one or more of our authors' newsletters, please visit **www.hayhouse.com®** or detach and mail this reply card.

Tune in to Hay House Radio to listen to your favorite authors: **HayHouseRadio.com®**

Yes, I'd like to receive:

☐ **a Hay House catalog** ☐ *The Louise Hay Newsletter*
☐ *The Christiane Northrup Newsletter* ☐ *The Sylvia Browne Newsletter*

Name _____

Address _____

City _____ State _____ Zip _____

E-mail _____

Also, please send:

☐ **a Hay House catalog** ☐ *The Louise Hay Newsletter*
☐ *The Christiane Northrup Newsletter* ☐ *The Sylvia Browne Newsletter*

To:
Name _____

Address _____

City _____ State _____ Zip _____

E-mail _____

To:

HAY HOUSE, INC.
P.O. Box 5100
Carlsbad, CA 92018-5100